# Parents Self-Help Guide Journeying Through Asperger/ Autism.

Written by Teresa Agresta
Edited/Proof read by Lauri Teschner

Farabee Publishing
P O Box 322, Chandler, Arizona, 85244
www.Farabeepublishing.com


Printed in the United States of America


Book Cover designed by: David Mor

# Table of Contents

## Bio of Author: Teresa Agresta

I was born in Schenectady, New York and have three beautiful sons that has inspired me to writing this book.

I never realized the journey I would be on when I had my children diagnose with ADHD and Asperger.

As a parent you want your child to excel in school and in life, so I understand the concerns, frustrations and overwhelming feelings you have in finding resources, and getting the support services in school for your ADHD and Autism child.

I never view my children diagnose as a disability but the wonderful gift that God has provided me.

## Introduction

There are many books about Asperger's Syndrome and Autism. Many of the books I have read teach parents about symptoms and go into detail about the disability.

My book will focus on several important issues such as temperament, sensory, social skills, evaluation, IEP, strategies, and transition services.

I understand the concerns; frustrations and the overwhelming feelings parents have in finding resources for their children. This is a journey you will be on from the day they are diagnosed until they reach adulthood.

The questions will become did I do everything possible in helping and supporting my child with this disability.

Honestly, the first instinct I had as a parent was to think it was possibly being a boy or he is going through the terrible two's, three's but as time prevailed, I found that I was making up excuses for my son behavior and delays.

Most parents read up on the different milestone's children accomplish, but today you need to educate on the warning signs for all kinds of disabilities.

I would like to tell you about my journey that has led me to writing this book. I would like to provide a personal perspective, resources and guide you in supporting your child who has been diagnosed with Asperger's Syndrome or Autism.

## My Journey With Asperger's Syndrome

When my son was born, he hit all of his milestones until he was two years old.  He wouldn't make eye contact, he would say only a few words, he had explosive tantrums, he would fixate on things, he loved to line up chairs, cars, and other items.

My instincts as a mom were to believe that boys are slow, they have delays and not to worry.  Some of his behavior could be justified because he was going through the terrible two's, then three's.

I came to the realization that some of the skills that my son was lacking were a real concern.  He could only communicate a handful of words, and I could not understand what he wanted which frustrated him.

He would have explosive tantrums; he would throw things at me, bite his brother, spit food out, and was unable to go to the store without having a tantrum.

The nights were long because he would scream during the night, and when he would wake up in the morning he would cry.  I was sleep deprived, and felt I was an awful Mom.

I needed answers about what was going on with him. My neighbor had a boy with Asperger's Syndrome. I started to talk to her about my son, and with the internet these days I was able to look up the symptoms of Asperger's Syndrome.

I quickly realized that he had some of the symptoms.

I took him to a child developmental physician, and they completed an evaluation on him. He was diagnosed with Asperger's Syndrome.

My heart was filled with disbelief, but deep down I knew it was true, and it was up to me to find out what resources he needed.

## What Is Asperger Syndrome?

Asperger's Syndrome has been defined as a developmental disorder that affects a child's social and communications skills. (Mayo Clinic, 2011)

I personally feel that it should be defined as a gifted person who has difficulty with social and communication skills.

### Symptoms

Some of the symptoms of Asperger's Syndrome children are as follow:

- ✓ Avoid Eye contact
- ✓ Head banging
- ✓ Lining up objects
- ✓ Awkward, repetitive gestures, or facial expressions
- ✓ Difficulty with peer relationships and social situations

- ✓ Inability to be empathetic or express their feelings
- ✓ Inability to read social cues
- ✓ Inability to sense other people's needs for personal space
- ✓ Late development of motor skills or a lack of physical coordination
- ✓ Fixated interest in one topic which they may talk about excessively
- ✓ Strong attachment to routine
- ✓ Difficulty changing from one task to another
- ✓ Sensitivity to sound, light, or touch
- ✓ Playing next to a child but not interacting

Children who have Asperger's syndrome may show any or all of these symptoms in various degrees. Sometimes the degree of an Asperger child is divided as low, medium or highly functional child.

Asperger's Syndrome or Autism may be the primary diagnosis but co-existing conditions such as ADHD, Depression, OCD, and Anxiety can exist.

If your child is 0 to 3 years old, I would recommend that you get Early interventions to come into your home to evaluate your child's developmental skills.

The services are free through your local state agency. Any child 4 years and older must go through the schools to get evaluated.

If your child is 4 or older you will need to write a letter to your school district advising them that you feel your child needs to be evaluated. Note the skills and delays in the milestones your child is experiencing difficulty.

These may include reading, writing, math or non-academic's like social, behavior or sensory issues. A complete psycho-educational evaluation should be completed on your child.

Usually, the journey begins by finding a neurological or child development physician.

These two types of physicians specialize in different types of disabilities.

They will do an assessment on your child's attention, memory, language and other skills pertinent to academic performance and behavior.

Once you obtain the diagnosis, then you likely begin with a variety of specialists.

## Different Types Of Specialist

These specialists will provide services on a weekly basis to strength their speech, sensory, and social skills. Some of these specialist services will overlap but they reinforce what is needed to improve their skills. The different types of Specialists are as follow:

Speech pathologist- works on speech and articulation:

- Occupational Therapist – achieve teaching how to dress, sensory issues, social skills
- Physical Therapy- helps with developing physical treatment such as muscles and coordination
- Special Education Teacher-Teaches strategies to academic learning, adapted equipment and materials, accessible settings, and other interventions designed to help learners with special needs achieve a higher level of personal self-sufficiency

## Speech Delays

One of the first symptoms I noticed in my son was how few words he was speaking. He would get very frustrated with me when I kept asking him, "What did you say," and he would throw tantrums.

If your child has a delay in speech and is saying a handful of words, this is a good time for him to be evaluated by speech pathologist to see how to improve his speech.

In order to have him communicate with me, I started to teach him sign language, so he could tell me what he wanted. Many of these sign languages you can look them up on www. youtube.com

- Yes,
- NO
- Eat
- Open
- Sorry
- Help

I was getting frustrated with the public schools that my son attended because of the three to one ratio for speech therapy.

He was only getting speech for 60 minutes per month. In my opinion, this was not meeting his needs. In addition to the school speech therapy, I also scheduled him with a private speech pathologist that my physician recommended.

You need pre-approval through your medical insurance before starting services.

I practiced speech exercises with my son to help him learn to enunciate the sounds that made his speech sound clearer.

I will demonstrate (below) how these exercises can help your child and then it is up to you to practice with your child at least 10 minutes a day. You will see the results.

## Speech Exercises

In order to make sounds clearer we need to strength the oral muscles in our mouth, so we can form the words to speak.

The following are exercises you can do in your home to strengthen your child's Oral muscle in their mouth.

- Sipping thick drinks like a smoothie or shake through a straw
- Gum Chewing
- Putting peanut butter or something of this texture on the roof of your mouth and let the tongue touch with roof of the mouth to get it off.
- Stick your tongue out and touch the left and right of your mouth
- Stick your tongue out six times
- Blowing a pinwheel or whistle
- Get a straw and blow up a small balloon and let them race across the room.
- Blowing bubbles with different types of instruments they offer for example pipe, wand etc.
- Saying OHH, AAH, EEE
- Board games that has pictures and the child needs to say the pictures.
- Say a word Hi, Bye, Ta, See, and have them repeat it back.

## Speech Articulation

Speech Articulation is how we produce sounds with speech. The common areas of speech problem are B, V, F, Th, S, Sh, CH you can type up a sheet with ten words on them and repeat the word 5 times. For example, She, Should, Shower, Thank You, Think etc.

I would have your child repeat them every single day until they are clear and precise when he says them to you.

The goal is to strength their oral muscles, so the sound comes out better when they are speaking. I know how frustrating it was for my son and I would see tantrums because I kept asking him please say that again. I hope these exercises help you.

## Sensory Issues

Sensory Defensiveness is in all of us. Think about how sounds, light, smell and how things feel on your feet, hands or body that makes us feel uncomfortable.

This sensory defensiveness become increasingly hypersensitive to Asperger's Syndrome and Autistic children.

You can have a mild to severe sensitivity to Sensory defensiveness. The range is as follow: (Wilbarger, 2001)

**Mild:** They are picky, over-sensitive, slightly overactive. Resistive to change or slightly controlling they can act mildly irritate by some sensation. They can be picky with their clothes and food.

**<u>Moderate</u>:** The child has difficulty with socializing and very aggressive or isolating themselves from peers. The have problems with attention and behavior in school.

**<u>Severe:</u>** These children usually have areas of delays in developmental, autism, or autistic behavior. Strong avoidance of some kids of sensation or he reverse, intense sensory seeking is common.

Sensory integration is the neurological process of organizing the information we get from our bodies and from the world around us for use in daily life.

Sensory integration provides a crucial foundation for later more complex learning and behavior.

For most children, sensory integration develops in the course of ordinary childhood activities.

The organization of behavior, learning and performance is a natural outcome of the process, as is the ability to adapt to incoming sensations. But for some children, sensory integration does not develop as efficiently as it should.

When the process is disorder, a number of problems in learning, development, or behavior may become evident to families and professionals. (Memorial Hospital ,2005)

Depending on the functionality of your child which can be low, medium or high, it will determine the degree of sensory your child will have and what needs to be worked on to strengthen their sensory needs.

**Vision-** Avoid eye contact, cannot stand to be in the light

**Audio**-difficult in loud noises such as people talking, music, vacuum cleaner

**Taste-** Different textures will bother them soft vs. hard food

**Smell** – High sensory to meats, and household products, perfumes etc.

**Body-** need to stand on tippy toes, need to be hugged, cannot stand certain clothes on themselves.

The question you are probably asking yourself is how do I help my child with some of these sensory issues.

You would get him evaluated by an occupational therapist. They would provide you with a sensory diet.

Sensory Diet is where you would put together activities that helps with some of the sensory issues he is having in school or in the home. There are a variety of exercise that your Occupational Therapist can suggest improving their sensory issues.

## Visual

When I would talk to my son, I would point to my noise with my index figure and tell him to look at me and tap my finger on my nose to get his attention. Do this every time you talk to your child and say good looking.

Doing this will teach them to look at you when you are speaking.  This becomes really important when they are communicating with others.

Most Asperger or Autistic children will look away because they become confused with looking and hearing when someone is speaking to them.  The child will look away in order to focus on one sense at a time.

## Audio

Often times you will see your child covering his ears because the sound is so loud to him it's like scratching your nails on a chalkboard.

The only way you can increase the awareness is to start low with sound and then in increments increase the volume to get use to louder sound.

Example turning on a radio and slowly increasing the volume on it.

## Taste

You will find out that some textures will make your child gag, vomit or just spit out food. I worked with my son to place a food that he had issues with such as hamburger.

I would place a couple of little pieces of hamburger for him to eat on a plate, with a piece of chocolate to get him motivated to try to eat a few pieces of hamburger.

Each day you increase the amount of food you give to him and then the reward is the cookie or food he loves. It truly works.

## Smells

Some children have a sensitivity to meat, fish, perfumes, household products. It can give them headaches, nausea, and gagging reflux.

Slowly, introduce different smells to your child to increase their awareness to get use to them.

## Body

Sometimes you will find that your son or daughter cannot stand the way clothes, socks, and other items feel on their skin.

I found that my son would hate a certain type of material for cloths that would drive him nuts or socks that feel funny on their feet. One of the ways to increase the feeling of these items is to do brushing.

Brushing is very important to children that have sensory issues. It's a soft sensory brush that you use to stroke in downward movement. You are going to brush their arms, legs back and feet.

Each body part should be brushed at least ten times. They will not like how the brush feels on their skin but in time they will get use to the brushing.

How many times a day depends on the severity of the child. I started brushing three times a day and then decrease it to two then one time before going to bed.

You can buy these sensory brushes on Amazon.com.

## Joint Compressions

Asperger's Syndrome and Autistic children will walk on their tippy toes or get very angry because they are looking for input that they are not getting. My son would get up in the morning and start crying for no good reason.

He would hop on my lap and want a hug. It wasn't until I learned that children with Autism seek certain input to feel whole again.

I would go through this routine of having him hop on my lap and give him his joint compression that would calm him down.

We would start our day and then when night time came, I would do Joint compressions with a massage to relax him.

You are going to start to do joint compressions on both of his legs, arms and core of the body. We will start with the feet and ankle, move to knee then the hip.

Do each of the legs first. Secondly, you will start with the hand and wrist, then elbow and arm and then shoulder.

Lastly go to the center of his chest and apply decompression. There are several You Tube videos of how to do the deep compressions. Five times for each area I have described above.

Asperger and Autism children seek these when they are at school, home and daycare. It would help them to learn and behave better.

Night time can be a big ordeal if they do not get the input they need to settle down, so they can fall asleep.

Most children have a hard time shutting their head off, so I would get some baby lotion and massage their feet, legs, arms, back and stomach. It's very relaxing to them and will fall asleep.

## Hands

I would find that when my son had ketchup or sticky substance on his fingers, he would get very upset. There are several exercises that you can do to help them with their tactile problem.

- Get plastic mat and spray shaving cream and hide animals and let them go find it
- Get finger painting and paper and let them use their fingers to paint you a picture.
- Get play dough and make different animals and characters out of it.
- Get plastic box and put different beans, and macaroni for sensory input
- Go to a sandbox and hide animals in the sand so they can find it.

## Over-Stimulated And Under-Stimulated

I remember when my son would come home from an outing and go into a meltdown. He would throw toys at me, scream, kick, and scratch me for over twenty minutes.

Afterwards he would calm down he would say I'm sorry and be this wonderful child for the rest of the day.

This behavior will occur because the child is over-stimulated or under-stimulated during the day. The best way to help him or her is to have him do a fun activity, read, watch TV or listen to music.

Sometimes they need their space to regroup from a busy day and this could take ten minutes up to an hour.

On the other spectrum they might be under-stimulated which means they have low brain activity.

Sometimes children need to get moving my doing some physical activity, so I recommend walking around, be a helper to get them moving around.

Depending the severity of their sensory needs you can do these exercises in your home or go to occupational therapy.

They will give you additional exercises to work on to overcome some of the sensory issues they have at this time that is affecting them with learning or behavior.

## Fixated On Objects

When I see my son fixated on an item I would redirect him to have an interest in other items. Many Asperger children will fixate on trains, cars and play with things.

I could remember how my son would open all the doors. I would close some of the doors and he would go in to a tantrum. It took some time, he got used to it.

If you find your child is fixated on an item, educate him on a new item and change thing up so he doesn't become so rigid with his behavior. It will get worse before it gets better but it's for their benefit.

## Transitional Anxiety

Many children often have difficulty going from one task to another. They start throwing tantrums in the store or going to school is a real hassle to get them in the car.

Here are some exercises that I did to help my child transit to different task easily.

- Take pictures of their daily routine and matte on a ring so they can see where they are going and what the routine is going to be daily. The old cliché a picture is worth a thousand words.
- Verbally in the morning going through the routine before they get to school or daycare, so they know what to expect. You will see as time goes by you will be doing this less. It's a skill they need to learn to adjust to change.
- Verbally start counting down the minutes until they need to change so I would tell my son we will be leaving for school in 15minutes, a little time go by and then I would say 10minutes, 5minutes then 3 minutes lets go to the school. It helps them make the transition.

## Sleeping Habits

Asperger's and Autistic children have a hard time falling asleep or staying a sleep.  I recommend routine, and consistency as much as possible.  Wake him up and put him to sleep at a certain time.

If they don't fall asleep, I recommend listening to the radio, read a bedtime story or some other routine that will get their mind off of things that they are thinking about.

Some providers recommend Melatonin 3 mg.  This is a natural herb that a child can take one hour before going to bed.  I am not a doctor, so please ask your pediatric physician before giving it to your child.

Another suggestion I recommend to getting your child falling asleep is a weighted blanket.  Weighted Blanket applies pressure, so the child feels grounded, and secure.

There is a company called Fun and Function that offers all types of sensory products.  There website is www.funandfunction.com  or http://www.sensorygoods.com/weightedproducts.aspx.

Many Asperger's children will have night terrors. It happens when children are sleep deprived so having a routine is very important.

They will be half awake with their eyes open screaming, yelling hysterically, and sweating.

These night terrors can last anywhere from five minutes to half an hour.

It is best to not wake them up quickly but just make sure they don't hurt themselves. I tried to talk in a nice tone and rub his back to slowly wake them up.

He will likely calm down and roll over to go to sleep. Don't be surprise if they don't remember that they were having a bad dream.

## PANDAS:

I was talking to my girlfriend about her son who was diagnosis with ADHD, OCD, PPD, etc. She was telling me how her son behavior was so defiant and angry, he would be chewing on cloths, WII controls, anything he could chew on.

I asked her if he was sick lately she said that he had a sore throat. I told her about **Pediatric Autoimmune Neuropsychiatric Disorder Associated with Streptococcus.**

Pandas is an autoimmune disease that effect part of the brain when a child has strep. Instead of a child having the infection in their tonsils it goes to their head.

A child behavior is extremely difficult to manage and high sensitivity to light, sound, and touch.

The symptoms to P.A.N.D.A.S.
- OCD -repetitive behaviors, excess fear of germs, hair pulling and eating disorders
- ADHD- fidgety, attention issues, irritability, sadness, emotional swings
- Sleep problems
- Sensory issues with chewy on items,
- Joint Pains

You can go to your pediatrician and ask them to have a blood test to see if he has Pandas.

Many physicians are misdiagnosis children with OCD and ADHD. They never consider that an infection is what causing the problem.

## Behavior Issues:

Different Types of Temperament.

Our children are wired the way they are and there is nothing you can do to change them. We need to accept them for who they are and try to work with their temperament.

Depending on the type of temperament your child has will depend on how you need to handle them when providing positive discipline. (Putnam, 2010)

There are three types of temperaments I am going to talk about in this book. They are Aggressive, Controlling, and Anxiety temperaments.

I have learned through my eight years of experience with Asperger's syndrome that we need not change the behavior but manage it.

These children have some skills that need to be developed and I am trying to teach you some positive discipline techniques that work if you follow the formula.

Aggressive temperament can be verbal as well as physical and the best thing to do is go into another room and ignore as long as it is safe.

If not just look away and do not make eye, contact it works like a charm. Children will use bad behavior to get your attention or to avoid consequences.

As a parent you do not want to reward them by giving them your attention when they use bad behavior.

When you tell them the behavior you want by telling them I would like to see you calm down and show respect. I will talk to you when you calm down.

**<u>Anxiety Temperament</u>** - Worry about everyday life events with no obvious reasons for worry. People with symptoms of generalized anxiety disorder tend to always expect disaster and can't stop worrying about what they have to do today.

**<u>Controlling Temperament</u>** become anxious when they feel they are not in control.

Strategies in handling the different temperament.

**Aggressive Temperaments** are born leaders. I feel it is important for us as parents to teach them about our leaders and what characteristics they should have if they were a leader.

Read books about Presidents and show how they are good listeners, communicate what they want, helping others, trustworthy, caring and how compassionate they are to people.

I would put aggressive children as a helper in home as well as in school.

**Anxiety Temperament-** One must face their fears in order to get over the hurdle of their fears. Many children might have the fear of weather or animals.

I would try to teach them about weather and then map out the weather for the week. If they learn how important it is for rain, so we can grow our food then the scariness will not be as bad.

If we learn about how sacred the cow is to some cultures. The importance of milk and meat that come from a cow. The cow is not as scary, and children need to use common sense to overcome their fears.

**Controlling Temperament-** The best way to get good results is to provide the child with a choice. Do you want to eat dinner or go to bed? They will pick the correct choice and if they don't follow through on consequence.

## Meltdowns And Tantrums

Many Asperger' Syndrome and Autistic children have meltdowns and tantrums. When a child is having a tantrum they are crying, kicking and screaming for a few minutes but gets over it after a few minutes.

A meltdown is when they are kicking and screaming, and emotionally cannot get in control. This will last ten minutes to an hour. When a child is in a meltdown, they are so upset about what is making them mad that they cannot regulate their emotions.

Here are a few techniques that I learned from Eric Putnam (2010), a license psychologist who told me not to discipline when my son is very angry.

I must wait until he is calm and then try to tell him what he should or shouldn't have done.

Some of these techniques are as follow:

(Putnam, 2010)

1. Be direct
2. Ignore
3. Provide choices
4. Tell a creative story and have them participate
5. Redirect their attention to a different topic so they get their mind off what is bothering them.

## Positive Discipline Techniques

Every parent's goal is to raise their child healthy and safe with good values. I would like to share how I use to focus on the bad behavior instead of focusing on the good behavior.

When your child is doing something wrong, tell them what the good behavior you are expecting. We seem to focus on the negative behavior, and this can lower our children self-esteem.

When my son was fighting with his brother over the Wii remote, he started to scratch and hit his twin in the face. I pulled him aside once he was calm and would listen and tell him the good behavior that I expected such as asking his brother nicely for the remote instead of hitting him.

I gave him a choice to apologize to his brother or go to his room. As I predicted he apologize to his brother. They hug, and life was grand again.

One of my favorite discipline books to read is 1 2 3 Magic by Thomas W. Phelan PhD.

He recommended that you give the child an opportunity to do the correct behavior. You count one, two, three, if the child doesn't follow through on the instruction then you give them a time out.

Depending on the age of the child will depend on the length of the time out.

Then you ask them again to do what you have requested, if they don't listen to your instruction, then you increase the length of time out until they complete your request.

This will take some time, but they will do what is told since kids hate to sit for a long time.

It is very important to show consistency when you discipline your child and following through with the consequences.

Children like to test the boundaries to see how far they can push your limits before they get punished. Bad behavior in a child needs to follow up with consequences.

The type of consequences will depend on the age of the child. Most children between 3-9 do not like to miss their shows or have snack time taken away.

Teenage children do not like to have their TV, Wii, Xbox, and cell phones taken away from them.

The big motivation is to find out what your child loves to do at home. You must follow through on the threat or they will not take you seriously. You can do it!

## Social Skills:

Asperger children have a difficult time making friends. They are looked at differently since they find it hard to interact with someone.

Most Asperger children play alone or will sit next to a child without interacting with anyone and play with their toys.

This is called parallel playing.

Some of my suggestions to strengthen their social skills are having play dates where you can help him on how to socialize with his peer. It helps when they can participate in sports, boys scout, chess club etc.

I read a book called Raising Your Child's Social IQ Stepping Stones to people skills for kids by Cathi Cohen (2000), which really helped me to guide my son in improving his social skills.

There are several areas that children are having a problem when it comes to socializing. Children have a hard time joining in, sportsmanship, communicating, coping with teasing, and resolve conflict and resolution.

There are several activities you can do with your children that will allow you to develop these skills. (Cohen, 2000)

## Joining In

Children need to understand that you have two choices when joining in to a group.

1. Ask to be join in the group
2. Automatic just join in the group

Many children have a hard time taking turns so playing board games such as trouble, I Spy, money game or Uno is a fun way to learn how to take turns in a small group of four people.

Sportsmanship is important concept to learn when you are young. There are always a winner and a loser.

Regardless who wins or loses I teach children that we should route the other team member on. Some Asperger or Autism children are so competitive at times that they need to lose gracefully.

To join in a group, one must do the following:
1. Wait your turn
2. Follow the rules
3. Stay Calm
4. Go with the flow
5. Be friendly

I really think it is important to talk to your child about when to join a group and when not to join in a group.

I would ask a child if you see someone being mean and is not following the rules, do you want to join in that group.

Hopefully, they would say no they don't, and they would find another group of kids to play with on the playground.

Some many Asperger and Autistic children have a hard time making friends I think it is very easy for them to be taken advantage of when playing with their peers.

My concern would be that they would get mixed in the wrong crowd of kids. This could be a bad influence on them.

I started early with my kids to tell them that drinking, smoking, drugs are bad choices. These choices can hurt your health and others.

## Communication

There are two forms of communication that children need to learn. Verbal and nonverbal communication.

Children need to use verbal communication to get what they want without crying, hitting, and taking toys when they want something.

When we are communicating to one another we need to:

1. Make eye contact to show we want to communicate
2. Show an interest in something you like to do, and ask questions to the other person
3.  Use a friendly tone in your voice
4. Make sure it's a two-way conversation

Many children can learn to verbally communicate by playing the "who am I" game. This game you have a hat that places a card above your head and the other person gives you clues to see if the item is a person, place or thing.

You can blind fold a child and have the other child direct them through a maze. Another way is to have them draw a picture and let them tell the story.

## Social Cues

Boundaries are about a person space and we need to give one another that space.

How do you feel when someone is really close to you?

1.  Use the hoola-hoop to show boundaries and try to have two people get close.
2.  Have a child on square and ask another person to move closer and see how the distant may be different with other kids.
3.  Stand towards each other and put our hands out to show distance.


Empathy is when we can put ourselves in a person place to see what they are feeling.

You can place different emotions in a hat and have them act out the emotion of happy, sad, angry, etc

I find when I use charades and Pictionary games Asperger and autism children can understand how to read someone body language is so important when interacting with other children.

I use charades to identify items, characters and shows. Sometimes there are books which identifies how a character is feeling in a book and the kids can tell you what they are feeling.

## Coping With Teasing

It is not easy to watch when your child is getting teased because they are different or may be physically or emotionally challenge.

Children may tease to be humorous or to be hostile which could include harassing.

1. When your child is being teased they should use humor to diffuse the situation.
2. Sometimes it is best to ignore the person who is teasing them and do not give them the attention they need.
3. You could agree to the facts. If the teaser says something about your freckles you can agree that you do have freckles.
4. I message is telling the teaser that I feel upset when you say I have ugly glasses.
5. You can use a compliment to diffuse teasing. if a child is teased about the way he runs, he can answer, "You are a fast runner."

## Conflict And Resolution

Many children today have a hard time attempting to resolve problems when they want to get what they want. Usually children will grab, cry and hit to get their way.

You could have the family get three cookies and two apples and each of you would ask how you would negotiate who gets the apple or cookie.

Jigsaw puzzles is a great way to problem solve and you could have a race to see who completes the puzzle first.

These are only a few suggestions to improve social skills with your child. I try to have my son attend a social skills group where he can interact with children his own age and learn some of these skills while having fun.

Many children organizations offer summer camp that will focus on art, drama, computers, and science.

## Diagnosis And Services In School

I took my son to a child psychologist when he was three years old because I saw signs of speech delayed, he wasn't socializing with other kids, meltdowns were occurring all the time, he was having a hard time going from one task to another.

His twin brother didn't have any trouble with these tasks, so I had a complete psychological evaluation done. He was diagnosis with Asperger's Syndrome.

The child development physician told me that they will send a report and I need to contact the school district to set up an IEP meeting. The physician has indicated that the School District will help your sons with his weakness and challenges.

I want to explain about the Complete Psychological Evaluation because it is very critical that you understand what is in this report.

This report will give the IEP team an understanding of the difficulties he has in school. Even though this report says he needs OT, PT, and Speech Therapy, the IEP team makes the final decision on your child's services.

The first step to getting your child evaluated in school is to put it in writing.   They have thirty days to respond to your request.  (See Example 1:)

## Complete Psychological Evaluation

The school should complete a psycho-educational evaluation, this often includes achievement and ability test. This test will measure your child's I.Q and cognitive abilities.

An example of cognitive abilities would be thinking, reasoning, and remembering.

Once you receive your diagnosis I would make sure that the report is broken down so that any areas below average will be obvious to you.

If your report does not show the subtest, it will not show where your child is below average.  Many times, these reports will show that he is average in communication because they combine the scores. (Ghose, 2013)

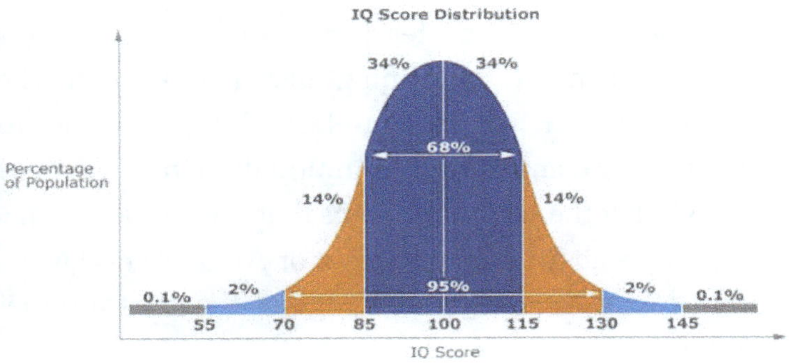


The chart above shows an IQ grading which shows average person would be in the 90-100 range.

Anyone that is below average will be in the 70-80 range. Anything above average which we would consider gifted would range in 101 plus range.

## What Is An IEP Vs. 504 Plan

A 504 Plan is a legal document that the school is being held accountable. This 504 Plan requires the school to make accommodations for your child that will help him with his education.

For example, having your child sit up front, having teacher check his organizer that assignments are being written down correctly, Notes are being giving to them on different subjects.

Individual Education Plan (IEP) is a legal document that the school is being held accountable that outline goals for your child.

Special Education teacher will help them in class with their notes, explaining instructions, a teacher assistant will help them with test taking, strategies for learning, and any other accommodation they will need.

One of the major problems that I see today as I talk to parents about their Asperger or Autistic child is that they do not have any knowledge on the laws and their rights.

## Rights as Parents

- ✓ The right to an appropriate evaluation (including academic and functional)
- ✓ The right to a free appropriate public education (FAPE)
- ✓ The right to have an Independent Education evaluation at the public expense. If you disagree with the school's evaluation.
- ✓ The right to an education in the least restrictive environment (LRE)
- ✓ The right to parental notice and participation
- ✓ The right to due process.

## IDEA 2004

The purpose of IDEA 2004 Law was to ensure children with disabilities receive an appropriate education through the school system. There are requirements that the school district must follow to be compliant.

The IDEA includes children with disabilities from 3 to 22 years old define in the following condition. These definitions may be altered by the Department of Education in your specific state. (2019, Department of Education)

Types of Eligibility:

- Mental retardation or Intellectual disability (mild, moderate and severe)
- Hearing Impairment
- Speech or language impairment
- Visual impairment
- Emotional Disturbance
- Orthopedic impairment
- Autism
- Traumatic brain injury
- Deaf-blindness
- Multiple disabilities
- Specific Learning disability
- Other health impairment which includes, ADD, ADHD, etc.

As an advocate, I find that schools are so focused on academics that they often do not focus on the nonacademic issues.

No one knows your child the way you do and it's really up to you to be an advocate for your child. It's hard for the school to understand what you go through at home with your child.

I recommend you start a binder and keep it updated on the assessments and evaluations you have from your IEP meeting.

Nonacademic and extracurricular services and activities may include counseling services, athletics, transportation, health services, recreational activities, special interest groups or clubs sponsored by the public agency.

You might be having issues with behavior, social skills, hygiene or some other life skills. Schools are not aware of these issues unless a parent brings these issues to their attention in the IEP meeting.

## Components Of IEP

In the Individual Education Plan there are seven components to an IEP Plan:
1. Present levels of achievement & functional performance
2. Annual measurable goals
3. How the goals will be measured & when progress will be reported
4. Special education and related services, modification, etc.
5. Extent the student will not participate with non-disabled peers
6. Accommodations necessary on state and district-wide assessments
7. Projected date services will begin

8.  Beginning at 16 years old postsecondary goals and transition
9.  How your child's needs for assistive technology will be met.

## IEP Meeting

After my son received his diagnosis, I looked at the evaluation report to see his weakness and strengths.

I requested to have an IEP meeting with the school district. Since my son had communication delays, sensory and social skills issues, he would need a speech pathologist, Occupational therapist, and special education services.

An IEP meeting is a team of professional and the parent, who develop and make decisions on services and accommodation their child needs to get a good education.

These meetings can be overwhelming when you have a teacher, psychologist, speech pathologist, special education, and occupation therapist attending these meetings.

It feels as if it is you against the rest of the school. It is so important that you tell them academic as well as non-academic issues.

For example, there could be social skills, behavior issues, and hygiene or any life skills they are having trouble with in school or home.

I feel it is very crucial to save assessments, emails, and any other documentation that will prove what problems he or she may be having in school.

- Bring a copy of the complete psychological evaluation
- Show the results on a bell curve to bring out their weakness
- Bring test results and homework grades to prove your point
- Print out any emails that you have with the teachers or school
- Bring up what you are seeing at home and your concerns.

## IEP Need Analysis Sheet

I recommend that you bring to your IEP meeting a need sheet of some of the issues you are seeing with his school work or challenges at home. A copy of an IEP Need Analysis Sheet will be at the end of the book you can use. (Example 3)

I have put together an IEP kit for you to use and hope you find it helpful as you partner up with the school district. You will need to get a binder and some tabs.

See Example 4. I recommend you have a collaborative approach when dealing with the school district.

I know how emotional I got when I sat down with six professionals at the table with my husband.  I feel intimidated when I go to an IEP meeting so I brought my IEP need analysis sheet.

Some suggestions about what could work for my son's challenges. I felt empowered as an advocate for my son's education.

## Accommodations On IEP

I knew my evaluation report recommended Occupational Therapy, Physical Therapy, and Speech Therapy for my son, but the school district felt speech therapy was needed for my son and Occupational therapy and physical

Therapy was not required for him. I had to take my son to an occupational therapist outside the school.  I talked to parents and my child development physician to get a list of resources.

We went twice of week for a year and it helped my son with his tactile and oral sensory issues.  School District have limited resources and parents need to find these resources in their community.

If you have your child at a private school like my son, please write a letter to your school district requesting to have your child evaluated for Speech or Occupational Therapy.

He may qualify to have someone come to the school to provide the service.

I know how hard it is to see your child struggle in the school environment.

I could remember how hard it was for my son to hear the loud fire alarm bells, overwhelmed with the school day, and transitioning from one task to another was difficult to watch.

I requested to have some accommodations with these skills.

Some of the accommodations that can help your child can be found on the internet. Susan Stokes, an autism consultant from Cooperative Exceptional Services had some Social and Academic skills goals. Social skills Goals (Stokes, 2011)

Goal: Johnny will develop his social skills and increase his interaction in school.

_______ Johnny will increase his/her social communication skills by interacting at age appropriate levels as demonstrated during classroom activities on three out of four days of interactions.

_______ Johnny will demonstrate the accurate use and understanding of statements and questions by increasing accurate use of these sentence forms 4 out of 5 opportunities to do so.

## Communication Goals:

Goal: Johnny will increase his verbal communication skills in school to identify his needs. (Stokes, 2011)

John will increase his verbal skills with his peer by asking questions and interacting with his peers 8 out of 10 opportunities.

## Transition Issues

Goal: John will regulate himself in classroom environment by using verbal and visual prompts. (Stokes, 1999-2011)

John will transition appropriately from tasks and activities in school environments 80% of the time given visual and verbal prompts.

John will accept changes in routine/schedule by exhibiting appropriate behaviors given visual and verbal cues 80% of the time.

## Accommodations In The Classroom

There is a difference between accommodations VS Modifications. An Accommodations is defined as altering the environment, or curriculum format in a regular classroom.

IEP or 504 Plan Accommodations

- ✓ Using extra time
- ✓ Testing in separate room.
- ✓ Using a computer to write
- ✓ Seating arrangements
- ✓ Notes will be provided by the Teacher
- ✓ Use Tape Recorder
- ✓ Oral Test

## Modifications In The Classroom

Modifications on IEP are changing the curriculum to meet the needs of the student's level of ability.

IEP Modifications
- ✓ Word bank for vocabulary word banks
- ✓ Less homework problems to do
- ✓ Projects instead of written reports
- ✓ Reworded Questions in simpler language

I recommend that you start to increase this modification of homework in high school. Your goal is to have him or her doing all of the problems by their Senior year.

Remember college will not modify how many problems they have in math or vocabulary in English.

## Suspensions From School:

Many children from kindergarten to high school are getting suspended because he or she have threatened to blow up the school or hit another peer in class.

Schools can suspend a child with a disability for up to 10 consecutive days (10 days in a row) for any violation of a school rule as long as that it is the same disciplinary action (and amount) applied to children without disabilities, except if the offense involves weapons, drugs or serious bodily injury.

## Functional Behavior Assessment

I see children having a hard time self-regulating their emotions in school. Many times, children are being suspended because they have threatened another child or want to blow up the building.

If you do not have a Behavior Intervention Plan on your IEP, then request to have an IEP meeting to have your child evaluated for his behavior issues.

The school will do a Functional Behavior Assessment. A Functional Behavior Assessment is a tool that psychologist or Behavior Specialist.

This is a process that they will document what becomes before the behavior (antecedent), the behavior the child is showing, and what happens after the behavior (consequences).

They accumulate this data from observing the child in classroom and interview the parents and teachers to see why the bad behavior is occurring. They can collect data for two to three weeks.

Once they have the data and decide what is causing the behavior issues, then they will put together with the IEP team a behavior Intervention plan. (Mauro, 2011)

Example of Functional Behavior Assessment: Page 79.

## Behavior Intervention Plan

A Behavior Intervention Plan is used to teach and reinforce positive behaviors. Typically, a child's IEP team develops the plan. It usually includes:

- Skills training to increase appropriate behavior
- Changes that will be made in classrooms or other environments to reduce and eliminate problem behaviors.

Why does a child show bad behavior?
- Escape/ avoidance
- Attention
- Expression of anger
- Frustration
- Seeking power / control
- Intimidation
- Sensory stimulation
- Relief of fear or anxiety
- Peer acceptance

Some Behavior Goals on an IEP would be as follow:

_____David will interact with his peer in a positive manner 8 out 10 times.

_____Gerry will raise his hand before speaking in class 8 out 10 times or 70%

_____Teresa will use appropriate language at all times and will show self-control 80%.

_____Alex will show 80% of the time good problem-solving skills in class.

_____Sandy will request a break when frustrated or upset by using the break card or verbalizing his needs 80% of the time.

Example of Behavioral Intervention Plan: Page 78.

## Multidisciplinary Evaluation Team (MET)

A team is put together to see if your son or daughter has a disability and therefore will qualify for special education services. They will review their strengthens and weakness of your child, academics test results, medical history, review any school records. Once the report is complete, they will have a meeting with the results of the MET.

## Transitions Services Out of High School

When your child reaches the age of 16 he will have an IEP plan that will provide a game plan to when he or she is transitioning out of high school and is going into the adult world.

I find this task to be one of the hardest things for me to accept as a parent.

I think how many tutors, occupational therapist, speech therapist, learning centers, psychologist and going to IEP meetings that have occurred over the past ten years of this child life time.

Now I come to a time where I need to give him the reigns to start advocating for himself.

One of the questions you are probably asking yourself is why should we worry about transition services?

There are statistics from (A New Era: Revitalizing Special Education for Children and Their Families, July 2002) which has indicated that higher rate of dropouts in high school, most children with disabilities earn less income then those who don't have disabilities.

Many children who have disabilities are unemployed or underemployed. This is why it is so critical to review what skills your child needs to learn before they graduate out of high school.

IDEA 2004 has defined Transition Services as follow:

The term *"transition services"* means a coordinated set of activities for a child with a disability that is designed to be within a results-oriented process, that is focused on:

- Improving the academic and functional achievement of the child with a disability to facilitate the child's movement from school to post-school activities,
- Including postsecondary education, vocational education, integrated employment (including supported employment); continuing and adult education, adult services,
- Independent living, or community participation;

Is based on the individual child's needs, considering the child's strengths, preferences, and interests;

Includes instruction, related services, community experiences, the development of employment and other post-school adult living objectives, if appropriate, acquisition of daily living skills and functional vocational evaluation.

The first step to transitioning from high school to the adult world I want you to have an idea what your child strengths and weakness.

You will find a parent Transition survey at the end of this book that will prompt you to ask your child when preparing for transitioning to college, vocational or on the job training.

Who is involved in the transitioning services? Its everyone from the parent, general educators, special education, Counselor, psychologist, Community agency, vocational educators, Transition personnel.

I know from experience it was hard for me to understand what to expect in a transition Service IEP. I want to outline some goals and objects that will help you through this process.

I want you to think about what your child strengths and list are them down on a sheet.

Now think about what skills do my child needs to learn before he leaves high school that will be critical for him to go to college, vocational, Job hunting etc.

Several things came to me as I was going to through the process with my eighteen-year-old son.
- ✓ Money management
- ✓ Teaching him how to set up doctors' appointments
- ✓ How to wash clothes and put them away
- ✓ Does he know how to make a meal for himself
- ✓ Decision making and goal setting

What areas must measurable post-secondary goals are being developed?
- ✓ Training and Education
- ✓ Employment
- ✓ Living skills

## Training and Education

One of the questions you will be asking your son or daughter are the types of post-secondary goals for themselves.

Will your child go to two-year college or four-year college? Will they want to learn a trade, so you might need information on vocational services?

Do they have interest in the military and if so, Army, Navy, Air Force and Marines?

They need a training program or learn on the job training?

<u>Goal:</u> Tyler will attend full-time at Chandler Gilbert Community College.

Goal: Student will acquire the skills to successfully transition to a two-year or four-year college/university.

Objectives:

___Student will enroll in academic classes that will prepare him/her for the educational challenges of postsecondary education.

___Student will schedule a visit with the Disability Services Coordinator for at least two colleges/universities to determine the levels of services available.

___Student will develop the skills to organize their work with efficiency.

___Student will develop strategies to enhance their study skills.

## Employment Goals and Objectives:

Goal: After Graduation Johnny will work full-time Computer application technician.

Goal: Student will complete a series of activities in order to prepare him/her to transition to full-time employment.

Objective:

___Student will develop a career portfolio to compile all vocational-related materials.

___Student will identify primary and secondary career goals comparing the qualifications necessary for success in such occupations with his/her own abilities.

___Student will complete RN (Name of Career) job-shadowing experiences related to expressed interests.

## Independent Living Skills Goals And Objective:

<u>Goal:</u> David will live in an apartment after graduation.

<u>Goal:</u> Student will acquire the necessary daily living skills to allow for independent functioning in a variety of environments (home, vocational and community).

<u>Objective:</u>

____Student will manage a budget, it will be based on a given dollar amount,

____The student will locate and purchase appropriate items in a store for meal preparation, clothing purchases, household and personal needs.

___Student will identify personal medical management needs (prescription, over-the-counter medicine, directions and safety of use).

___Student will maintain a clean bathroom – based upon specific teacher criteria.

## Community Participation Goals and Objectives

Goals: Student will acquire the necessary skills to access the community with independence (and/or specified levels of support).

<u>Objectives:</u>
Establishing a checking and saving account and completing transactions at a bank.

___Student will read and follow directions, maps, signs and transportation schedules.

Student will participate in extracurricular activity/clubs in the school and community.

___Student will learn the skills to access appropriate medical care (calling doctors to make appointments).

___Student will identify leisure activities that they can enjoy in their free time.

## Transition Assessments

There is not a one size fits all assessments that will show your child's learning style, interest, and accommodations are needed.

There are formal and informal assessments.

<u>Formal Assessments:</u>
- ✓ Standardized achievement tests
- ✓ Intellectual functioning assessment
- ✓ Adaptive behavior scales
- ✓ Aptitude tests
- ✓ Personality scales
- ✓ Self-determination scales
- ✓ Pre-voc/employability scales
- ✓ Interest Inventories

<u>Informal Assessments</u>
- ✓ Interest inventories
- ✓ Skills inventories
- ✓ Situational observations
- ✓ Situational assessments
- ✓ Interviews

When you go to your IEP Transition Service meeting you should know the following: please look at my sample form at the end of the book to show you what an IEP Transition Services should include.

- ✓ Transition plans should include an appropriate course of study for the student while he/she is still in high school
- ✓ Community service agencies and/or adult agencies like Vocational Rehabilitation should be invited to participate in the students' IEP meeting (if appropriate)
- ✓ There should be someone assigned to each goal to show who is being responsible for that goal.

Transition meeting meet annually but you can request a meeting anytime. Transition goals can be changed and updated.

Transition plans are unique for each student. The student's interests, strengths, and preferences should be clearly noted.

I have learned through my own experience with my son that you should not wait until they are seniors to think about college.

I find the biggest problems as parents we think about today and never think about tomorrow. I want you to start thinking about the bigger picture in five years where you would like to see your child academics and non-academics goals.

I have provided a Parent Survey for Transitional Services (Example 5) for you to use when you start thinking about what your child is going to do when they graduate from high school.

## Talents

All children have special talents that need to be noticed and nurtured, so they will do well in school and in their daily lives.

Parents have an important role in helping their children develop these talents by working with them at home.

Talents can be defined as being good at a sport, playing a musical instrument, having the ability to be kind and funny. These are a few suggestions that can help you see what talents your child have in themselves.

Whatever talents your child has been given, praise them for it when you catch them in the moment.

Teachers should have an awareness of these talents to motivate and build your child's self-esteem in school. (Putnam, 2010)

## Self Esteem And Motivation In Children

I feel it is important for parents to have an awareness of our children's self-esteem. Many children that have Asperger's Syndrome or Autism get picked on and bully at school.

As a mother who has an Asperger's child, I am concern he will have low self-esteem.

He has a difficult time making friends because of his weakness in socializing. I make sure he is involved in sports, boys' scouts, chess, and other events that he excels in to improve his confidence and social skills.

Also, I would praise him for his academic achievements or his accomplishments in drawing or music to boost his self-esteem.

Self-esteem is the way we feel about ourselves. I think it's important for parents to encourage positive feeling in our children.

When I hear my son say he is stupid, or he cannot make friends, I tell him we all have things to improve about ourselves.

Remember, to have the I can do attitude and drill it into them until they start believing. The only way a child or ourselves can increase our self-esteem is by doing.

I would provide chores list or make him set the table even assist me in my social skills group to build his self-esteem.

Motivation can be difficult if children do not want to try something new. Asperger children like to stay in routine and not venture out of their comfort zone.

I would make my son go to birthday parties and sports events to get him out to socialize. If he needs some motivation I would set up a rewards system to have him do his homework or behave in a positive manner.

These rewards will depend on the age of the child. Some parents believe kids should not be rewarded all the time to do what's expected of them.

I believe if it motivates him to be positive and do the right thing, I am fine with it. Once he learns the right behavior or make better choices I would back off on the rewards.

## Diet and Drinks

I know that diet and sugar drinks can affect a child's behavior. These are common sense things we have been hearing since we were kids. Diet alone is not going to get rid of Asperger's Syndrome or Autism.

There are many factors why children have these disabilities today. I blame it on the environment, the food we eat, immunizations, and genetics.

There is not one element that is causing the increase in Asperger's and Autism.

I believe we can help our children in improving their temperament by watching what they put into their bodies. As parents we can monitor the amounts of sugar and carbohydrates that they intake on a daily basis.

Everything should be done in moderation when it comes to food. Some kids need to eat smaller meals because they burn through food quickly.

Hyperglycemic children will have their sugar up and down so if they try to eat less sugar and carbohydrates in their diet and smaller meals this could help them with their bad behavior.

Some doctors recommend for us to eat organic food to get more nutrients in our diet. I try to eat as health as possible but it's difficult when we are on the go so much.

Many doctors that I have visited which were holistic or naturopathic have recommended to take a multiple vitamin. Our diets are lacking protein, magnesium, folic acid, omega 3, and zinc.

Since Asperger's Children has sensory to foods they will not like the taste or texture of the vitamin.

My son would like to drink a shake, so I would make a protein drink. These drinks come in chocolate or vanilla and I add fruit to flavor it up for him.

Be careful on what brand you buy because some protein drinks are made for adults.  I started out with Ensure and then as my son got older, I gave him Isagenix.

There are energy drinks that are all natural like Vemma that I heard about from Dr. Oz on TV. Vemma has no sugar or caffeine in it, but only comes in orange flavor.

If your child has a dislike for orange drinks, then you might want to see if sprouts or other organic markets carry something similar in a different flavor. Soda and sugar juices are the worst drinks we can give to our children who have behavior issues.

## Gluten Free Food

I tried to put my son on a gluten free diet and found it impossible to do. He didn't like the taste of the bland food.

Many children can get tested for gluten by taking a blood test.  I believe you need to give it a try if your child is constipated and has stomach aches when he eats.

You can have an allergy to gluten and the test results say that you don't.  Speaking from experience with myself who tested positive with Gluten free.

I feel better when I do not eat a lot of carbs in my diet. You need to read the labels on boxes, cans, Teresa Welshand packages.

Sprouts and Whole Foods which are located on the west coast has all their products marked Gluten free. I find them very pricey but well worth the benefit if I don't eat wheat in my diet.

I would try this for a month with your child and see if he is feeling better or not.

## Conclusion:

I hope this self-help guide was informative and resourceful to you. I am not a psychologist, Speech pathologist, or Occupational Therapist but a parent who has been on this journey for the past nine years.

I know how it feels to be a single parent, and the frustration of working with your spouse or significant other who may feel differently about what is happening to your child.

You need to understand that you are not alone and that I have talked to many parents who are on this journey too.

The only way we can set our children up for success is by providing extra support in the home and finding outside community organization and advocating for services in school that can provide some of these services to support the skills are children need to learn.

## Books To Read

- ✓ Emotional Intelligence By Daniel Goldman
- ✓ Louder than Words by Jenny McCarthy
- ✓ Raising Social IQ Stepping stone to people skill for kids by C. Cohen, (2000)
- ✓ Out of Sync child by Carol Stock Kranowicz
- ✓ 123 Magic by Thomas Phelan

# Example 1: Letter To Request To Get Your Child Evaluation:

Your Name
Street Address
City, State, Zip Code
Daytime telephone number

Name of Principal or Special Education Administrator
Name of School
Street Address
City, State, Zip Code

Dear (Principal's or Administrator's name),

I am writing to request that my son/daughter, (child's name), be evaluated for special education services. I am worried that (child's name) is not doing well in school and believe he/she may need special services in order to learn. (Child's name) is in the (_ ) grade at (name of school). (Teacher's name) is his/her teacher.

Specifically, I am worried because (child's name) does/does not (give a few direct examples of your child's problems at school).

Thank you for your prompt attention to my request.

Sincerely,


Your name


cc: Your child's principal (if letter is addressed to an administrator) your child's teacher(s)

## Example 2: Needs Analysis for IEP Meeting

**Eligibility:**

- ☐ Autism
- ☐ Multiple Disabilities
- ☐ Developmental Delay (ages 3-10)Multiple Disabilities Severe Sensory Impairment
- ☐ Emotional DisabilityOrthopedic Impairment
- ☐ Hearing ImpairmentPreschool Severe Delay
- ☐ Other Health Impairments –
    - ☐ ADHD
    - ☐ Speech/Language Impairment
    - ☐ Specific Learning DisabilityTraumatic Brain Injury
    - ☐ Visual Impairment

**Academic Learning problems**

- ☐ Math problems
- ☐ Sight words
- ☐ Writing

**Attention Issues:**

- ☐ Take test in quiet room
- ☐ study skills/organization skills
- ☐ Daydreaming
- ☐ Going from one task to another
- ☐ Short term memory

**Audio Processing**

- ☐ Re-direction with instruction
- ☐ Reading Comprehensive

**Body**
- ☐ Cannot stand someone touching them
- ☐ Need to be hugged
- ☐ Cannot stand clothes or socks on them
- ☐ Walking on their toes

**Behavior Issues**
- ☐ Aggressive- overly Explosive
- ☐ Anxiety
- ☐ Controlling
- ☐ fixation on items
- ☐ Easily Frustrated
- ☐ Repetitive activities or motions
- ☐ Meltdowns or Tantrums
- ☐ Cannot regulate emotions
- ☐ Coping skills

**Coordination**
- ☐ clumsy, trips, runs into things
- ☐ Slumps
- ☐ Hard to run

**Food problems**
- ☐ Gag on different textures
- ☐ Issues with Smells of perfumes, meat, house products

**Hyperactivity**
- ☐ climbing on furniture
- ☐ Cannot sit still

## Impulsiveness
- ☐ Talking out loud
- ☐ Cannot take turns
- ☐ Hits or touch people
- ☐ chew things
- ☐ cannot stand getting dirty
- ☐ Problem Solving

## Sensory Issues

### Visual
- ☐ Flipping of letters and words
- ☐ Copy from board to paper
- ☐ Can't make eye contact

### Audio
- ☐ Loud Noises
- ☐ Delay in responding to instruction

## Social Skills
- ☐ Joining in
- ☐ Taking turns
- ☐ Delay in Verbal Communication
- ☐ Nonverbal communication
- ☐ Teasing
- ☐ Resolving Conflicts

## Speech
- ☐ nonverbal- understanding social cues
- ☐ Verbal cannot talk clear

# Example 3: IEP Binder Information:

| Section 1—IEP / 504 Plan Child's most current SIGNED IEP or 504. | Section 2— Assessments (Child Study Team) | Section 3— Independent Evaluations | Section 4— Correspondences to School | Section 5— Correspondences from school |
|---|---|---|---|---|
| All other IEP's should be filed away in a separate binder as reference. | _Educational | Child's profile "successes" | _ Document phone calls | _ Document phone calls |
| Suggest current and previous year of the IEP. | _ Functional | What they can do vs. what they need help doing. | _ Letters | _ Letters |
|  | _ Social |  | _ E-mails | _ E-mails |
|  | _ Psychological |  | _ Notes | _ Notes |
|  | _ Speech |  |  |  |
|  | _ Occupational Therapy |  |  |  |
|  | _ Physical Therapy |  |  |  |

## Example 4:  Parent Transition Survey

Student: _______________________________

Date: _______________________________


Please add any comments or concerns that you feel will assist the IEP team in making decisions for the Individual Education Program (IEP). (Fournier, L.L. M.E. Morningstar, I. Crawford, J. Scarff & M. Blue-Banning, 2014).

## Area 1: Post-Secondary Education

My son/daughter intends to go on to post-secondary education or training as indicated:

_____ 4-year College _____ Community College

_____ Vocational/Technical School _____ Other

_____ My son/daughter does not intend to go on to post-secondary education

_______________________________________________

Comments_________________________________________


## Area 2: Vocational Training

My son/daughter has successfully completed course work in the following vocational areas:

_____ Family and Consumer Sciences

_____ Computers

_____ Construction Trades

_____ Business

_____ Health Studies
_____ Industrial Arts
_____ Photography
_____ Graphic Arts
_____ Auto
_____ Other:

---

## Area 3:  Career And Employment

My son/daughter has had the following work experiences:
_____ Volunteer employment _____ Full or part-time employment
_____ On the Job training
_____Military


My son/daughter requires IEP team assistance in the following areas:
_____ Career exploration
_____ Identification of personal interests, values, and skills
_____Career planning
_____Conducting a job search
_____Completing applications for employment
_____Job interviewing skills
_____Preparing resumes
_____Developing pre-employment behaviors: following directions, staying on task, completing tasks, locating materials, dress and grooming issues, etc.

____Developing employment behaviors: attendance, punctuality, use of equipment, independent work habits, completing assigned tasks accurately, increasing productivity, etc.

____ On the job training with a job coach

____ Other:

_______________________________________

Comments:_______________________________

_______________________________________

## Area 4: Continuing And Adult Education

My son/daughter requires assistance from the IEP Team in the following:

____Identifying possible continuing education options

____Information about Adult Education Programs

____Information about GED Preparation Programs

____ Referral to an adult agency for continuing education

____ Other

Comments:_______________________________

_______________________________________

## Area 5: Adult Services

My son/daughter is currently connected to the following community agencies:

____Division of Vocational Rehabilitation (DVR)

____Division of Developmental Disabilities Services (DDDS)

____Social Security Administration

____Other
_______________________________________

My son/daughter requires IEP Team assistance in the following:

____Identifying appropriate agencies for support services

____Referral to an adult service provider

____Assistance in completing an application for services

____Other

Comments:_______________________________________
_______________________________________

## Area 6: Independent Living Skills

My son/daughter has age appropriate skills in the following areas:

____ Budgeting

____ Maintenance of a household

____ Cooking

____ Self-help (grooming, dress, hygiene)

____ Communication skills

____ Recreation/leisure skills

____ Community safety

____ Caring for personal health

____ Accessing medical assistance

____ Self-advocacy

____ Shopping

____ Money skills

____ Use of banking services

____ Use of credit
____ Accessing transportation services
____ Personal relationships
____ Caring for others (babysitting, parents)
____Making friends
____Accessing community services
____Other___________________________________

____________________________

My son/daughter needs IEP Team assistance in the following areas:

____Money management (banking, credit, budgeting)
____Personal care (dress, grooming, hygiene)
____Household management (bills, rent, household maintenance, cleaning, etc.)
____Community safety
____Personal relationships (making friends, sex education, etc.)
____Caring for others (parenting skills, family relationships, dating, marriage)
____Communication skills
____Social skills
____Recreation/Leisure skills
____Shopping Skills
____Self Advocacy (accessing assistance in legal, medical, financial areas)
____ Other

_________________________________________

## Area 7: Recreational Activities

My son/daughter accesses the following community organizations:

____Religious organization of choice

____Athletic club

____Hobbies, and interest

____Swimming

____School athletics/clubs/extracurricular activities

____Other

My son/daughter uses the following transportation:

____Drives self

____Community public transportation

____Taxi service

____Bicycle

____Walks


My son/daughter needs IEP Team assistance in the following areas:

____Identifying community organizations and activities

____Participating in school activities

____Using community skills

____Developing recreation/leisure skills

____Referral to a community service provider

____Other

Comments:_________________________________________

_______________________________

# References

A New Era: Revitalizing Special Education for Children and Their Families, July 2002. From: http://ectacenter.org/~pdfs/calls/2010/earlypart c/revitalizing_special_education.pdf

Arizona Department of Education of Exceptional Services: Transition Services (2010). Retrieved From: www.azed.gov/special education.

Cohen, C., (2000). Raising your children social IQ stepping stones to people skills for kids. Advantage Books, MD.

Delaware Department of Education (2012). Parent transition survey. Retrieved From: http://www.doe.k12.de.us/infosuites/students_family/specialed/files/speced_DEparentsurvey rev.pdf

Encyclopedia Children's Health (2012). (Psychological tests - meaning, definition, purpose, description, risks. Retrieved From: http://www.healthofchildren.com/P/Psychological-Tests.html#b#ixzz1luqaFJXI.

Ghose,T.,(2013)http://ca.news.yahoo.com/simple-vision-test-predicts-iq-160717367.html.

Mauro, T., (2011) Behavior intervention plan; children with special needs. About.com. Retrieved, From:http://specialchildren.about.com/od/behavioranddiscipline/g/BIP.htm .

Mayo Clinic Staff (2011, June 9). Asperger syndrome definition. Retrieved From: http://www.mayoclinic.com/health/aspergers-syndrome/DS00551.

Memorial Hospital, Inc. (2005). Parent's Guide to Understanding Sensory. Retrieved From: http://memorialhospital.org/SensoryIntegration.htm

Fournier, L.L. (Revised 2014). Parent Transition Survey. From Parent Transition Survey by M.E. Morningstar, I. Crawford, J. Scarff & M. Blue-Banning (1994). Adapted with permission. Retrieved From: http:transitioncoalition.org

Putnam, E., (2010), Challenge temperaments, independence behavior coaching. www.mybehaviorcoach.com

Siegel, M. L., (2011) The Complete IEP guide how to advocate for your special ed child. 7th edition. Nolo Trademark, CA.

Stokes, S., (2011). Examples of IEP goals and objectives suggestions for autism children. Cooperative Education Services, Agency No.7, WI. Retrieved From www.naset.org/.../Examples_IEP_Goals_Objectives_for_ASD.pdf.

Wilbarger, P., MED, OTR and Wilbarger, J. L., MS, OTR (2001). "Sensory defensiveness in children aged 2-12, an intervention guide for parents and other caretakers" Avanti Educational Programs.

# Behavioral Intervention Plan

Date: 2/1/98

Student Name: Case 3 - Ed          ID: 0003          DOB: 5/3/82          Case Manager: Mr. Roberts

| Behavior Number(s) | Expected Outcome(s) Goal(s) | Intervention(s) & Frequency of Intervention | Person Responsible | Goal/Intervention Review Notes |
|---|---|---|---|---|
| 1 | A. During free time, interacts with other students and staff 90% of the time.<br><br>B. Goes to lunch in the cafeteria without supervision 90% of the time.<br><br>C. On task 90% of the time.<br><br>D. Completes assigned work 90% of the time. | A. Social work involvement for referral for family counseling focused on realistic expectations of student performance. Ongoing until counseling is started.<br><br>B. Daily monitoring medication compliance and effectiveness.<br><br>C. Bibliotherapy for parents. Ongoing.<br><br>D. Teach the student alternative positive self-statements and appraisals. Daily, as needed.<br><br>E. Reinforce positive self-statements, attention to school work, and initiating social interactions. Daily, as needed<br><br>F. Weekly group instruction of combating irrational and self defeating thinking in special education classroom. | Social worker<br><br><br>Nurse, Teacher<br><br>Parents<br><br>Teacher<br><br>Teacher<br><br>Teacher | 4/1/98 - Showing improvement to 60% on Goal A. Showing improvement on Goals C and D. Little change in Goal B. Social worker made contact with parents, but they are resistant. Continue efforts on intervention A and C. Intervention F seems to be very effective. Need to increase treatment integrity on intervention E. Goal B is unique that it is not in the classroom. Need to interview student to better understand social problems outside of class. |

* Review Codes: GA = Goal Achieved | C = Continue | DC = Discontinue          Expected Review Dates: 4/1/98 | 5/1/98 | __________

Signatures: ________________  ________________  ________________  ________________  ________________

________________  ________________  ________________  ________________  ________________

Page ____ of ____

Student: _______________________ Grade _______ School: _______________________ Date: __________

Participants: _______________________________________________________

This FBA will be utilized for:   ☐ Programming purposes   ☐ IEP requirements

**1** Describe the behavior/incident in observable terms:

___________________________________________
___________________________________________
___________________________________________
___________________________________________
___________________________________________
___________________________________________
___________________________________________
___________________________________________
___________________________________________
___________________________________________
___________________________________________
___________________________________________
___________________________________________
___________________________________________
___________________________________________

**2** If the above statement addresses multiple behaviors, identify the ONE BEHAVIOR to be targeted for intervention:

___________________________________________
___________________________________________
___________________________________________
___________________________________________
___________________________________________

**3** Other medical/mental conditions that may contribute to target behavior: __________________________

___________________________________________
___________________________________________
___________________________________________

**4** ANTECEDENTS

What is likely to "set off" or precede the problem behavior?  WHEN is the problem behavior most likely to occur?

☐ Morning — approximate time(s) ____________
☐ Afternoon — approximate time(s) ____________
☐ Before/after school   ☐ Lunch/recess
☐ *Time of day does not seem to affect this behavior*

WHERE is the problem most likely to occur?
☐ Reg. Ed. classroom        ☐ Spec. Ed. classroom
☐ Hallways        ☐ Cafeteria
☐ _______________________________
☐ *Location does not seem to affect this behavior*

During what SUBJECT/ACTIVITY is the problem behavior most likely to occur?
☐ Subject(s) _______________________
☐ Unconstructed activities   ☐ Seatwork
☐ Group Activities   ☐ Transitions
☐ Lesson presentations   ☐ Task explanations
☐ _______________________________
☐ *Subject/activity does not seem to affect this behavior*

The PEOPLE that are present when the problem behavior is most likely to occur include:
☐ Teacher        ☐ Classmates
☐ Other Staff        ☐ Other peers
☐ _______________________________
☐ *Subject/activity does not seem to affect this Behavior*

Are there OTHER EVENTS or CONDITIONS that immediately precede the problem behavior?
☐ A demand or request
☐ Unexpected changes in schedule or routine
☐ Consequences imposed for behavior
☐ Comments/teasing from other students
☐ _______________________________

When is the student most successful?  When DOESN'T the problem behavior occur? _______________

___________________________________________
___________________________________________
___________________________________________
___________________________________________

**5** CONSEQUENCES

What "payoff" does the student obtain when she/he demonstrates the problem behavior?

The student GAINS:
☐ Teacher/adult attention
☐ Peer attention
☐ Desired item or activity
☐ Control over others or situation
☐ Self Stimulation
☐ _______________________________

The student AVOIDS or ESCAPES:
☐ Teacher/adult attention
☐ Peer attention
☐ Non-preferred activity, task or setting
☐ A difficult task or frustrating situation
☐ _______________________________

What has been tried thus far to change the problem behavior?
☐ This is a first occurrence and will be addressed through this FBA and Behavior Intervention Plan.
☐ Implemented rules and consequences for behavior are posted.
☐ Implemented behavior or academic contract.
☐ Implemented home/school communication system.
☐ Adapted curriculum — How? _______________
____________________________________
☐ Modified instruction — How? _______________
____________________________________
☐ Adjusted schedule — How? _______________
____________________________________
☐ Conference with parents — Dates? _______________
____________________________________
☐ Sent student to office — Dates? _______________
____________________________________

Notes:

Notes:

Notes:

# Parents Self Help Guide ADHD and ADD Children.

Written by Teresa Agresta

The events are true, but the names have been changed for privacy reasons.





ISBN: 978-1-64713-642-0 ebook: 978-1-64921-824-7

Farabee Publishing
P O Box 322, Chandler, Arizona, 85244
www.Farabeepublishing.com

Printed in the United States of America

*Book Cover designed by: David Mor*

Table of Contents

## Bio of Author: Teresa Agresta

I was born in Schenectady, New York and have three beautiful sons that has inspired me to writing this book.

I never realized the journey I would be on when I had my children diagnose with ADHD and Asperger.

As a parent you want your child to excel in school and in life, so I understand the concerns, frustrations and overwhelming feelings you have in finding resources, and getting the support services in school for your ADHD and Autism child.

I never view my children diagnose as a disability but the wonderful gift that God has provided me

## Introduction:

Many of the books I read on ADHD and ADD disabilities provides you with symptoms, and technical terms that are hard to read.

I understand the concerns, frustrations and overwhelming feelings you have in finding resources, and getting the support services in school for your ADHD and ADD child.

Today it seems that we not only have to understand the different stages of child development but have an education on different types of disabilities our children can developed.

My book will focus on several important issues such as temperament, sensory issues, social skills, psychological evaluation, IEP VS 504 Plan, strategies in school and home, Transition Services in high school, and diet.

I would like to tell you about my journey that has led me to writing this book. I would like to provide a personal perspective, resources and guide you in supporting your child who has been diagnosed with ADD and ADHD.

## My Journey with ADHD:

My son accomplished all his child development skills up to kindergarten. When he was in first grade, he had problems with reading comprehension and writing skills.

He was having a hard time memorizing his multiplication and spelling words. Homework was so frustrating for us because he didn't want to do it.

Studying for a test was hard for him because he would need a week to study. He was disorganized and couldn't copy from the chalkboard to his notebook.

I knew I had to do something for him since his self-esteem was very low and motivating him to do school work was impossible.

I received a diagnosis of ADHD inattentive by his child development physician. I could remember how overwhelmed I was at my first IEP Meeting.

There were teachers from each class, of Math, Science, Social studies, English, Special Education teacher, case manager, and counselor around this long table and I felt out numbered.

They allowed him some accommodations on his IEP in school. He had notes that were giving to him and they help him with organization skills.

In New York State we had a teacher assistant assigned to him in science and math class.

There was no communication to the parent as to how to help him with studying or strategies with his short-term memory issues.

I spent lots of money on tutors and sat twice a week in my car while he was being tutored on the Wilson program to help him learn his sight words.

I had reward charts and motivated him with extra time on the TV or Xbox. Whatever it took for him to apply himself I did it.

As he was getting older in his teens it was most challenging because you can only motivate so much and then it's up to him to apply himself.

We would have Thursday night for reviewing his grades and homework assignments to see if he would be allowed to go out on the weekend.

We use the car, cell phone, XBOX, and IPOD as a motivator to get his work done and put time in for studying.

**If he didn't study or homework was missing,** I would follow through on consequences. He is a very compassionate, loving, caring, creative, people-oriented person.

I had to teach him about money management, interviewing techniques and how to find a job.

Our journey to adulthood is approaching quickly so don't think about what you need to do today but continue to look down the path of tomorrow. It comes sooner than you think.

## Types of ADHD

I know it's hard for parents to determine if their child has ADHD or ADD.  Most children are very active and cannot sit down for two minutes.

I kept making excuses and telling my son he needs to apply himself.  Some of the old cliché about boys being just boys can only go so far when you see them struggling academically and having trouble paying attention can be the deciding factor of get him or her evaluated. (CHADD, 2012)

The Children and Adults with Attention Deficit/Hyperactivity Disorder (CHADD) defines the following symptoms for **ADHD - Inattentive** Type:

- Fails to give close attention to details or makes careless mistakes.
- Difficulty sustaining attention. (daydreams)
- Does not appear to listen or follow directions
- Struggles to follow multiple instructions.
- Difficulty with organization.
- Avoids or dislikes tasks requiring sustained mental effort.
- Easily distracted.
- Forgetful in daily activities.

Children who are hyperactive run like every ready battery. While children who are impulsive react without thinking.

You can have a child with combination of these two types of disabilities. CHADD defines the following symptoms **for ADHD**

**Hyperactive/Impulsive:**

- Fidgets with hands or feet or squirms in chair.
- Has difficulty remaining seated.
- Runs around or climbs excessively.
- Has difficulty engaging in activities quietly.
- Talks excessively
- Blurts out answers before questions have been completed.
- Has difficulty waiting or taking turns.
- Interrupts or intrudes upon others.

**Co-existing Condition:**

Many children can be diagnosis with ADHD but have a co-existing condition that is occurring at the same time.  The most common disorders that occur with ADHD are:
- Oppositional defiant disorder
- Depression or bipolar disorder
- Anxiety disorders
- Learning disabilities

Oppositional Defiant disorder (ODD) is a behavioral disorder that children will show aggressive and defiant behavior towards others.

Children will frequently have tantrums, question rules, and blame others for their own mistakes.

I recommend parents to take a parent class on challenging behaviors or work with a behavior coach who can show you some techniques that will support this challenged behavior in the home. (AACP,2010)

**Depression** is feeling of sadness, angry, withdrawn and thoughts of death or suicide. Many children will show a few symptoms but its best to seek a professional child psychiatrist to evaluate the situation.

**Bipolar Disorder** symptoms are different in children then adults. Children will have temper tantrum, aggressive behavior, irritability, mood swings, and like gory or morbid topics.

**Anxiety Disorder** is the fear and worrying of daily activities at school and home. Children need to learn some techniques to help their anxiety.

Some deep breathing and help him or her rationalizing their fears will help but should seek professional help from school psychologist or child psychologist.

**Learning Disability** is very common in ADHD and ADD children. Some of the symptoms you will find in children are difficulty in reading comprehension, have a hard time following direction, and trouble remembering sounds of words.

If you see difficulty in reading, writing and math, have your child evaluated by the school psychologist or child development physician.

## Temperament

Our children are wired the way they are and there is nothing you can do to change them. We need to accept them for who they are and try to work with their temperament.

Depending on the type of temperament your child has will depend on how you need to manage them when providing positive discipline.

There are four types of temperaments I am going to talk about in this book. They are aggressive, controlling, anxiety temperaments, and stimulated seekers. (Putnam, 2010)

I have learned through my ten years of experience with ADHD that we need not change the behavior but manage it.

These children have some skills that need to be developed and I am trying to teach you some positive discipline techniques that work if you follow the formula.

**Aggressive Temperament** will be very verbal as well as physical angry and frustrated towards you. They have a hard time keeping friends. They use negative behavior for attention or avoidance of consequences.

**Anxiety Temperament** - Worry about everyday life events with no obvious reason. They have overwhelming feeling of threat, disaster, and bad events.

People with symptoms of generalized anxiety disorder tend to always expect disaster and can't stop worrying about what they have to do today.

**Controlling Temperament** become anxious when they feel they are not in control.

**Stimulated Seekers-** These are the ADHD children who are always bored. They cannot keep enough interest in a task long enough. Most ADHD children will achieve a task and want to move on to the next thing. (Putnam, 2010)

## Strategies In Handling The Different Temperament

Aggressive temperament children can be verbal as well as physical towards you when they want your attention or trying to avoid consequences. The best way to handle this type of temperament is to avoid confrontation. (Putnam,2010)

I would have your child sit in a room with no TV or toys. This is not punishment but a place they can calm themselves.

It will not benefit you or the child if they are so angry that they cannot hear what you are trying to tell them. Depending on the age of the child, you should remove yourself from the room.

Go into another room to avoid eye contact and ignore them as long as the child is showing aggressive behavior.

If the child gets up and follows you into the other room, I would have them sit down and you will need to stand over them with your hand on their shoulder or just put your hand out in front of them and do not make eye contact with them. This works like a charm.

**Aggressive Temperaments** are born leaders. I feel it is important for us as parents to teach them about our leaders and what characteristics they should have if they were a leader. (Putnam,2010)

Read books about Presidents and show how they are good listeners, communicate what they want, helping others, trustworthy, caring and how compassionate they are to people. I would put aggressive children as a helper in home as well as in school.

Children will use bad behavior to get your attention or to avoid consequences.

As a parent you do not want to reward their bad behavior by giving the attention, they want from you.

Instead, you will tell them the behavior you want them to show towards you by telling them to calm down and show respect.

You will talk to him or her when he or she is calmed down. Go in to the room every 5 to 10 minutes and praise him or her for calming down.

Once they calm down you will ask them why they got upset or what they needed and talk in a nice voice. If an apology is needed or consequence needs to be done, then you need to follow through with it.

**Anxiety Temperament** - Children worry about everyday life events with no obvious reasons for worrying.

Anxiety children might need a visual aid to show their schedule and you can put this up to be reviewed daily. Also, you can verbally tell them their schedule for the day. (Putnam,2010)

Deep breathing exercises help calm them down and just do these ten times. It will relax them.

Sometimes redirecting them to focus on another topic will help them get pass their anxiety.

One must face their fears in order to get over the hurdle of their fears. Many children might have the fear of weather or animals.

I would try to teach them about weather and then map out the weather for the week.  If they learn how important it is for rain, so we can grow our food then the scariness will not be as bad.

If we learn about how sacred the cow is to some cultures. The importance of milk and meat that come from a cow.  The cow is not as scary, and children need to use common sense to overcome their fears.

**Controlling Temperament** become anxious when they feel they are not in control. The best solution for them is to provide them with two choices and have them pick one.  (Putnam,2010)

The best way to get good results is to provide the child with a choice.  Do you want to eat dinner or go to bed?  They will pick the correct choice and if they don't follow through on consequence.

**Stimulated Seekers-** ADHD and ADD children have a hard time focusing on one task for a long time and are ready to move to the next task.

As parents we need to develop that skill, so they can entertain themselves for a while, so we can get our work done.

It is not our job to find things for them to do but to encourage them to develop this skill over time.

Some suggestions would be to have them sit down and write a list of things they like to do and let them check it off as they do them. I would set a timer, so they know when to move on to the next task.

## Positive Discipline Techniques

Every parent's goal is to raise their child healthy and safe with good values. I would like to share how I use to focus on the bad behavior instead of focusing on the good behavior.

When your child is doing something wrong, tell them what the good behavior you are expecting. We seem to focus on the negative behavior and this can lower our children self-esteem.

When my son was fighting with his brother over the Wii remote, he started to scratch and hit his twin in the face.

I pulled him aside once he was calm and would listen and tell him the good behavior that I expected such as asking his brother nicely for the remote instead of hitting him.

I gave him a choice to apologize to his brother or go to his room. As I predicted he apologized to his brother. They hug, and life was grand again.

One of my favorite discipline books to read is 1 2 3 Magic.by Thomas W. Phelan PhD.

He recommended that you give the child an opportunity to do the correct behavior.

You count one, two, three, if the child doesn't follow through on the instruction then you give them a time out.

Depending on the age of the child will depend on the length of the time out.  Then you ask them again to do what you have requested, if they **don't listen** to your instruction, then you increase the length of time out until they complete your request.

This will take some time, but they will do what is told since kids hate to sit for a long time. It is very important to show consistency when you discipline your child and following through with the consequences.

Children like to test the boundaries to see how far they can push your limits before they get punished.

Bad behavior in a child needs to follow up with consequences. The type of consequences will depend on the age of the child.

Most children between 3-9 do not like to miss their shows or have snack time taken away.

Teenage children do not like to have their TV, Wii, Xbox, and cell phones taken away from them.

The big motivation is to find out what your child loves to do at home.  You must follow through on the threat or they will not take you seriously. You can do it!

## Strategies In The Home

Some of my tips will be helpful in the home when your child is trying study, organize, memorize and trying to pay attention. I have used some of these with my children and hope it will be helpful to you.

### Executive Function

Executive Function is defined as the mental process to organizing, planning, memorizing, attention span and strategizing. These are problems that your ADHD and ADD child will have when they are in school. (Ehmke, 2019)

### Organizational Tips

- Get a school organizer where they can write down all their homework assignments. Each day go over what he has and check it off that it is done.
- Place a bulletin board in their bedroom to show what they have for sports, projects, appointments, and homework assignments.
- Homework chart will show Monday through Friday and each of the subjects they have in school. This can be laminated so you can get an erasable marker that they can cross off each assignment. Exhibit 1

## Chunking

When doing homework break it in to segments so that he can focus on one subject at a time.

Let him do homework for 15 minutes then provide a break since attention span is so short.

Yes, this takes a long time but it's better to have quality work then having him fly through it to get it done.

## Rewards

I would have a goodie jar to motivate him to get through the homework.  They need to have a goal to get the task done.

I would set up a reward chart Monday through Sunday to show accomplishments if they do their homework and work with you give them a star or sticker depending on the age of the child.

As they get older I use the point system so points add up to reward.

If your son or daughter is in their teens then use a jar and when they receive a certain amount of points then they can get an inexpensive reward such as extended time TV, curfew, Xbox etc.

## Paying Attention

If he or she is daydreaming a lot have, them chew gum it grounds them when doing homework.

Have a set area to have him do homework where he won't get distracted from people or TV.

You can have them sit on exercise ball or ridged disc to ground them, so they can pay attention to what they are doing.

Give them breaks between homework assignments.

You can get the exercising ball and disc seat at a Sporting Goods place or go www.funandfunctions.com

Set a timer on the stove when they do homework, so they know when to take a break.

**Short Term Memory Issues**

Some ADHD children will have very short memory issues. Studying for a test will be very difficult.

Repetition is the key to getting information into long term memory. There are certain memory techniques that will work such as: (Bridger,2008)

**Association-** Get a visual picture to make association to the word.

**Acrostic-**Making up a sentence such as Every Good Boy does fine to remember notes EGBDF

**Acronym-** "HOMES" to remember the names of the Great Lakes: Huron, Ontario, Michigan, Erie, and Superior

**Rhyme-** Thirty days past September, April June and November the rest has 31 except February which has 28.

Taking a test is difficult do when you have short term memory issues. You need to have a week in advance and everyday review the material, so it becomes familiar to you.

Most ADHD and ADD are visual learners so you can be creative with clay, crayons and other activities to get the concept down.

## Studying

ADHD children have no motivation skills internally, so it is going to take external motivation to get these kids to complete any task.

You can create a reward chart which you mark daily, so they can see they are working toward something.

You deduct points if they do not follow through on task. Once they achieve the points give the reward.

Teenagers are very difficult to motivate. I would have rules in the house that in order to get Xbox, cell phone, car etc. they need to do the following through on homework, chores, and task that they need to get done.

# Self Help Guide to ADHD and ADD

I would hang up a board in their room that they can write their assignments and teach them how to organize themselves. It will be a key to setting them up for success.

See if the teachers would allow a tape recorder so you can revisit some of the lectures you had on a particular subject.  This would be a great review for your son or daughter to keep it fresh in the head.

Concept mapping- This is a tool for ADHD children to use when they need to take notes. There are three reasons why it works for them.

First, ADHD children are visual learners and a lot of words in a book are very overwhelming when you have to memorize information.

Concept mapping breaks things down so they can get key concepts and relationships.  (Franz, 2019)

Example of Concept Mapping: Exhibit 2

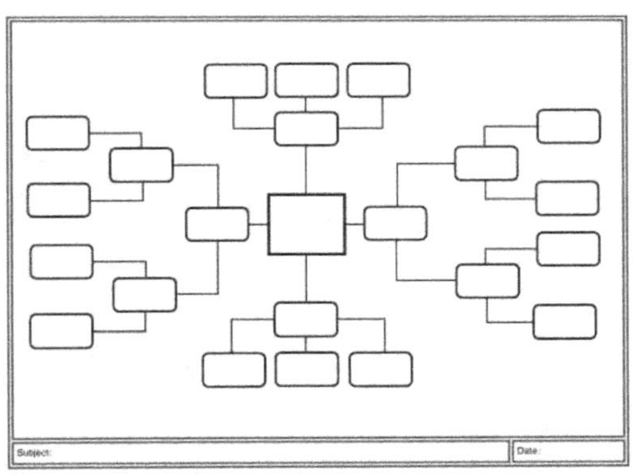

## Venn Diagram

Venn Diagram are used to show an understanding of similar and difference. You can write details that tell you how the subjects are alike in the center. Write details that tell how the outer circles are different. Exhibit 3

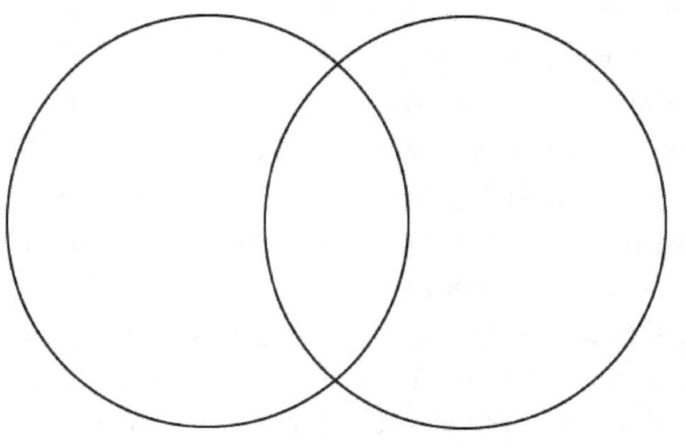

## Sensory Integration

Sensory integration is the neurological process of organizing the information we get from our bodies and from the world around us for use in daily life. (Wilbarger, 2001)

Sensory integration provides a crucial foundation for later more complex learning and behavior.

For most children, sensory integration develops in the course of ordinary childhood activities. The organization of behavior, learning and performance is a natural outcome of the process, as is the ability to adapt to incoming sensations. (Wilbarger, 2001)

But for some children, sensory integration does not develop as efficiently as it should. When the process is disorder, a number of problems in learning, development, or behavior may become evident to families and professionals.

Depending on the functionality of your child which could be low, medium or high, it will determine the degree of sensory your child will have and what needs to be worked on to strengthen their sensory needs. (Wilbarger, 2001)

**Vision**- Avoid eye contact, cannot stand to be in the light.

**Audio**- difficult in loud noises such as people talking, music, vacuum cleaner

**Taste**- Different textures will bother them soft vs. hard food

**Smell** – High sensory to meats, and household products, perfumes etc.

**Body**- need to stand on tippy toes, need to be hugged, cannot stand certain clothes on themselves.

The question you must be asking yourself is how do I help my child with some of these sensory issues.

**Sensory Diet** is where we put together activities that a child needs when they are hyperactive, and impulsive.

Depending on the functionality of your child which could be low, medium or high, it will determine the degree of sensory your child will have and what needs to be worked on to strengthen their sensory needs. (Wilbarger, 2001)

**Vision**- Avoid eye contact, cannot stand to be in the light

Audio-difficult in loud noises such as people talking, music, vacuum cleaner

**Taste**- Different textures will bother them soft vs. hard food

**Oral**- Chew their clothes and other items such as pencils etc.

**Smell** – High sensory to meats, and household products, perfumes etc.

**Body**- need to stand on tippy toes, need to be hugged, cannot stand certain clothes on themselves.

The question you must be asking yourself is how do I help my child with some of these sensory issues.

**Sensory Diet** is where we put together activities that a child needs when they are over-stimulated or under-stimulated.

Children can get overstimulated and need some downtime or under-stimulated they need some arousal to get them going.

If you go to the end of my book there is an example of questions to see about your child sensory issues.

**Audio**

Many times, you will see your child covering his ears because the sound is so loud to him it's like scratching your nails on a chalk board.

The only way you increase the awareness is to start low with sound and then in increments increase the volume to get use to louder sound.

For example, turning on a radio and slowly increasing the volume.

**Taste**

You will find out that some textures with your child will make them gag, vomit, or just spit it out at the table.

I worked with my son to place a food that he had issues with such as hamburger. I would place a couple of little pieces of hamburger for him to eat on a plate, with a piece of chocolate to get him motivated to try to eat a few pieces of hamburger.

Each day you increase the amount of food you give to him and then the reward is the cookie or food he loves. It truly works.

**Oral**

You will find your child biting on their clothes or put items in their mouth to chew.

This is an oral sensory need that they will need help with.  There are several ways to help them with this need is to have them chew gum, suck thick liquids through a straw, and by different types of chewy that goes on your wrist, pencils, or just to bite.

It beats them having unhealthy items such as the Wii remote to chew.

The following are exercises you can do in your home to strengthen your child's Oral muscle in their mouth. (McKissick & Segura, 2000)

- Sipping thick drinks like a smoothie or shake through a straw.
- Gum Chewing.
- Putting peanut butter or something of this texture on the roof of your mouth and let the tongue touch with roof of the mouth to get it off.
- Stick your tongue out and touch the left and right of your mouth.
- Stick your tongue out six times.
- Blowing a pinwheel or whistle.
- Get a straw and blow up a small balloon and let them race across the room.
- Blowing bubbles with different types of instruments they offer for example pipe, wand etc.
- Saying OHH, AAH, EEE
- Board games that has pictures and the child needs to say the pictures.
- Say a word Hi, Bye, Ta, See, and have them repeat it back.

## Smells

Some children have a sensitivity to meat, fish, perfumes, household products.

It can give them headaches, nausea, and gagging reflux. Slowly, introduce different smells to your child to increase their awareness to get use to them.

You can blind fold and have them guess the items that they can smells such as candles, spices, and herbs.

## Body

Sometimes you will find that your son or daughter cannot stand the way clothes, socks, and other items feel on their skin.

I found that my son would hate a certain type of material for cloths that would drive him nuts or socks that feel funny on their feet.

One of the ways to increase the feeling of these items were to do brushing.

Brushing is very important to children that have sensory issues. It's a soft sensory brush that you use to stroke in downward movement.

You are going to brush their arms, legs back and feet. Each body part should be brushed at least ten times.

They will not like how the brush feels on their skin but in time they will get use to the brushing. How many times a day depends on the severity of the child.

I started brushing three times a day and then decrease it to two then one time before going to bed. You can buy these sensory brushes on Amazon.com.

## Joint Compressions

ADHD and ADD children get very hyperactive and Impulsive. They can have behavior issues if they don't get the input that they need and can come across as a trouble maker. (Wilbarger, 2001).

I have seen children jump, run and climb over furniture. They have so much energy that they don't know what to do with it.

You are going to start to do joint compressions on both of his legs, arms and core of the body.

We will start with the feet and ankle, move to knee then the hip. Do each of the legs first.

Secondly, you will start with the hand and wrist, then elbow and arm and then shoulder.

Lastly go to the center of his chest and apply decompression. There are several You Tube videos of how to do the deep compressions. Five times for each area I have described above.

### Hands

I would find that when my son had ketchup or sticky substance on their fingers, he would get very upset. There are several exercises that you can do to help them with their tactile problem.

- Get plastic mat and spray shaving cream and hide animals and let them go find it
- Get finger painting and paper and let them use their fingers to paint you a picture.
- Get play dough and make different animals and characters out of it.
- Get plastic box and put different beans, and macaroni for sensory input
- Go to a sandbox and hide animals in the sand so they can find it.

## Over-Stimulated And Under-Stimulated

I could remember when my son would come home and go into a meltdown.  He would throw toys at me, scream, kick, and scratch me for over twenty minutes.

Afterwards he would calm down he would say I'm sorry and be this wonderful child for the rest of the day.

This behavior will occur because they are over-stimulated or under-estimated during the day.  The best way to help him or her is to have him do a fun activity, read, watch TV or listen to music. (MS, OTR,2001).

Sometimes they need their space to regroup from a busy day and this could take ten minutes up to an hour.

Some ADHD and ADD children might be under-stimulated which means they have low brain activity.

Sometimes children need to get moving by doing some physical activity, so I recommend walking around, be a helper to get them moving around.

Depending the severity of their sensory needs you can do these exercises in your home or go to an occupational therapy.

They will give you additional exercises to work on to overcome some of the sensory issues they have at this time that is affecting them with learning or behavior.

## Social Skills

Today, many ADHD children have co-existing conditions like oppositional defiant disorder have difficult time making friends.

They are looked at differently since they find it hard to interact with someone. Some of my suggestions to strengthen their social skills is to start to have play dates where you can help him on how to socialize with his peer.

It helps when they can participate in sports, boys scout, chess club etc.

I read a book called *Raising Your Child's Social IQ Stepping Stones To People Skills for Kids* by Cathi Cohen, that really helped me to guide my son in improving his social skills.

There are several areas children are having a problem when it comes to socializing.

Children have a hard time joining in, sportsmanship, communicating, coping with teasing and resolve conflict and resolution.

There are several activities you can do with your children that will allow you to develop these skills.

## Joining In

Children need to understand that you have two choices when joining in to a group.

1. Ask to be join in the group
2. Automatic just join in the group

Many children have a hard time taking turns so playing board games such as trouble, I Spy, money game or Uno is a fun way to learn how to take turns in a small group of four people.

Sportsmanship is important concept to learn when you are young. There are always a winner and a loser. Regardless who wins or loses I teach children that we should route the other team member on. Some children are so competitive at times that they need to lose gracefully.

To join in a group, one must do the following:
- Wait your turn
- Follow the rules
- Stay Calm
- Go with the flow
- Be friendly

I really think it is important to talk to your child about when to join a group and when not to join in a group.

I would ask a child if you see someone being mean and is not following the rules, do you want to join in that group.

Hopefully, they would say no they don't, and they would find another group of kids to play with on the playground.

Many ADHD and ADD children have a hard time making friends I think it is very easy for them to be taken advantage of when playing with their peers.

As a parent, I would be concern with whom they would be socializing with the wrong crowd of kids. This could be a bad influence on them.

I started early with my kids to tell them that drinking, smoking, drugs are bad choices. These choices can hurt your health and others. (Fuerst, Mark,2016)

## Communication

There are two forms of communication that children need to learn. Verbal and non- verbal communication. (Cohen, Cathi, 2000)

Children need to use verbal communication to get what they want without crying, hitting, and taking toys when they want something.

When we are communicating to one another we need to

- Make eye contact to show we want to communicate
- Show an interest in something you like to do, and ask questions to the other person
- Use a friendly tone in your voice
- Make sure it's a two-way conversation

Many children can learn to verbally communicate by playing the "who am I" game. This game you have a hat that places a card above your head and the other person gives you clues to see if the item is a person, place or thing.

You can blind fold a child and have the other child direct them through a maze. Another way is to have them draw a picture and let them tell the story.

**Social Cues**

Boundaries are about a person space and we need to give one another that space.  How do you feel when someone is really close to you?

- Use the hoola hoop to show boundaries and try to have two people get close.
- Have a child stand on square and ask another person to move closer and see how the distant may be different with other kids.
- Stand towards each other and put our hands out to show distance.

Empathy is when we can put ourselves in a person place to see what they are feeling.

You can place different emotions in a hat and have them act out the emotion of happy, sad, angry, etc.

I find when I use charades and Pictionary games children can understand how body language is so important when reading children.

I use charades to identify items, characters and shows. Sometimes there are books which identifies how a character is feeling in a book and the kids can tell you what they are feeling.

## Coping With Teasing

It is not easy to watch when your child is getting teased because they are different or may be physically or emotionally challenge.

Children may tease to be humorous or to be hostile which could include harassing.

- When your child is being teased they should use humor to diffuse the situation.
- Sometimes it is best to ignore the person who is teasing them and do not give them the attention they need.
- You could agree to the facts. If the teaser says something about your freckles you can agree that you do have freckles.
- I message is telling the teaser that I feel upset when you say I have ugly glasses.
- You can use a compliment to diffuse teasing. if a child is teased about the way he runs, he can answer, "You are a fast runner."

## Conflict And Resolution

Many children today have a hard time attempting to resolve problems when they want to get what they want. Usually children will grab, cry and hit to get their way.

You could have the family get three cookies and two apples and each of you would ask how you would negotiate who gets the apple or cookie.

Jigsaw puzzles is a great way to problem solve and you could have a race to see who completes the puzzle first.

These are only a few suggestions to improve social skills with your child. I try to have my son attend a social skills group where he can interact with children his own age and learn some of these skills while having fun.

Many children organizations offer summer camp that will focus on art, drama, computers, and science.

## Getting Services In School

When you feel your child is having problems in school. You can write a letter to your school district indicating what troubles your child is having in school.

The school has sixty days to respond to your letter. The school will provide an I.Q test to see if your child is performing at their grade level.

Depending on what issues your child is having, in school will determine what type of test and evaluations that will need to be done.

If the school thinks that your child is having a hard time learning, then they will provide Psycho-educational evaluation.

## Diagnosis And Services In School

I took my son to a child psychologist when he was nine years old because I saw signs of reading comprehension problems, disorganization and having a hard time remembering information on a test.

Once he was diagnosis with ADHD inattentive, the child development physician sent me a copy of the report.

I had to contact the school district to set up a meeting to determine if he would get an IEP or 504Plan.

The child development physician has indicated in their evaluation what weaknesses my child had in reading, writing, math, audio and visual issues.

I want to explain about the Complete Psycho-educational Evaluation because it is very critical that you understand what is in this report.

This report will give the IEP or 504 plan team an understanding of the difficulties he or she has in school.

Even though this report says he needs OT, PT, and Speech Therapy. The IEP team makes the final decision on your child's services.

The first step to getting your child evaluated in school is to put it in writing. They have sixty days to respond to your request. Exhibit 4 letter to the school.

## Complete Psychological Evaluation

The school should complete a psycho-educational evaluation, this often includes achievement and ability test. This test will measure your child's I.Q and cognitive abilities which is audio processing, visual processing, short-term, working memory, and long-term memory.

The school psychologist will conduct an I.Q test, but I recommend having them do a complete psycho-educational evaluation.

Once you receive your diagnosis, I would make sure that the report is broken down so areas below average will be obvious to you.

If your report does not show the subtest, it will not show where your child is below average. Many times, these reports will show that he is average in communication, but he might have a high score in nonverbal communications and low score in verbal communication. (Ghose,2013)

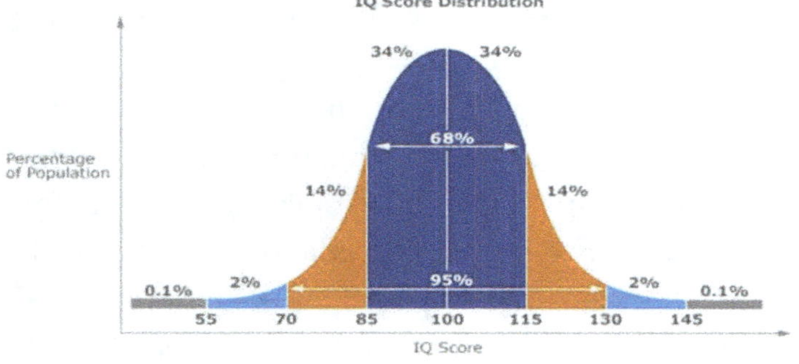


The chart above shows an IQ grading which shows average person would be in the 90-100 range.

Anyone that is below average will be in the 70-80 range. Anything above average which we would consider gifted would range in 101 plus range.

## School Requesting For An Evaluation

It is really important as a parent to be an active participate into the IEP meeting.

What is an IEP vs. 504 plans?

A 504 Plan is a legal document that the school is being held accountable that outlines goals for your child.

This 504 Plan requires the school to make accommodations for your child that will help him with his education. For example, having your child sit up front, having teacher check his organizer that assignments are being written down correctly. Notes are being giving to them on different subjects.

Individual Education Plan (IEP) is a legal document that the school is being held accountable that outline goals for your child.

Special Education teacher will help them in class with their notes, explaining instructions, a teacher assistant will help them with test taking, strategies for learning, and any other accommodation they will need.

One of the major problems that I see today as I talk to parents about their ADHD or ADD children, they do not have any knowledge on the laws and their rights.

## Rights As Parents

✓The right to an appropriate evaluation (including academic and functional)
✓The right to a free appropriate public education (FAPE)
✓The right to have an Independent Education evaluation at the public expense. If you disagree with the school's evaluation.
✓The right to an education in the least restrictive environment (LRE)
✓The right to parental notice and participation
✓The right to due process.

## IDEA 2004

The purpose of IDEA 2004 Law to ensure that children with disabilities receive an appropriate education through the school system. There are requirements that the school district must follow to be compliant.

The IDEA includes children with disabilities from 3 to 22 years old define in the following condition. These definitions may be altered by the Department of Education in your specific state. (Arizona Dept of Education)

**Types Of Eligibility:**

- Mental retardation or Intellectual disability (mild, moderate and severe)
- Hearing Impairment
- Speech or language impairment
- Visual impairment
- Emotional Disturbance
- Orthopedic impairment
- Autism
- Traumatic brain injury
- Deaf-blindness
- Multiple disabilities
- Specific Learning disability
- Other health impairment which includes, ADD, ADHD, etc.

As an advocate, I find that schools are so focused on academics that they often do not focus on the nonacademic issues.

No one knows your child the way you do and it's really up to you to be an advocate for your child. It's hard for the school to understand what you go through at home with your child.

I recommend you start a binder and keep it updated on the assessments and evaluations you have from your IEP meeting.

Nonacademic and extracurricular services and activities may include counseling services, athletics, transportation, health services, recreational activities, special interest groups or clubs sponsored by the public agency.

You might be having issues with behavior, social skills, hygiene or some other life skills. Schools are not aware of these issues unless a parent brings these issues to their attention in the IEP meeting.

## Components Of IEP:

In the Individual Education Plan there are seven components to an IEP Plan:

1. Present levels of achievement & functional performance
2. Annual measurable goals
3. How the goals will be measured & when progress will be reported
4. Special education and related services, modification, etc.
5. Extent the student will not participate with non-disabled peers
6. Accommodations necessary on state and district-wide assessments
7. Projected date services will begin
8. Beginning at 16 years old postsecondary goals and transition
9. How your child's needs for assistive technology will be met.

Optional Components:(Siegel,2011)

1.  The IEP may include specific teaching methods, particular class subjects,
2.  Any behavior strategies to reinforce positive behavior.
3.  The language needs of children with limited English.
4.  Communication needs with deaf and hard of hearing children.

**IEP Meeting**

After my son received his diagnosis, I looked at the evaluation report to see his weakness and strengths. I requested to have an IEP meeting with the school district.

Since my son had communication delays, sensory and social skills issues, he would need a speech pathologist, Occupational therapist, and special education services.

An IEP meeting is a team of professional and the parent who develop and make decisions on services and accommodation their child needs to get a good education.

These meetings can be overwhelming when you have a teacher, psychologist, speech pathologist, special education, case manager, psychologist, and occupation therapist attending these meetings.

It feels as if it is you against the rest of the school. It is so important that you tell them academic as well as non-academic issues.

For example, there could be social skills, behavior issues, and hygiene or any life skills they are having trouble with in school or home.

I feel it is very crucial to save assessments, emails, and any other documentation that will prove what problems he or she are having in school.

- Bring a copy of the complete psychological evaluation
- Show the results on a bell curve to bring out their weakness
- Bring test results and homework grades to prove your point
- Print out any emails that you have with the teachers or school
- Bring up what you are seeing at home and your concerns.

## IEP Need Analysis

I recommend that you bring to your IEP Need Analysis of some of the issues you are seeing with his school work or challenges at home.

A copy of an IEP need analysis will be at the end of the book you can use. (Exhibit 5)

I recommend you have a collaborative approach when dealing with the school district. I know how emotional I got when I sat down with six professionals at the table and my husband and I feeling intimidated when I go to the next IEP meeting with my IEP need analysis and have some suggestions about what works for my son's challenges.

I felt empowered and advocated for my son's education.

## Accommodations On IEP

I knew my evaluation report recommended Occupational Therapy, Physical Therapy, and Speech Therapy for my son, but the school district felt speech therapy was needed for my son and Occupational therapy and physical Therapy was not required for him.

I had to take my son to an occupational therapist outside the school. I talked to parents and my child development physician to get a list of resources.

We went twice of week for a year and it helped my son with his tactile and oral sensory issues. School District have limited resources and parents need to find these resources in their community.

I know how hard it is to see your child struggle in the school environment.

I could remember how hard it was for my son to hear the loud fire alarm bells, overwhelmed with the school day, and transitioning from one task to another was difficult to watch.

I requested to have some accommodations with these skills.

There is a difference between accommodations VS Modifications.

Accommodations is defined as altering the environment, or curriculum format in a regular classroom.

**IEP Accommodations**

- ✓ Using extra time
- ✓ Testing in separate room.
- ✓ Using a computer to write
- ✓ Seating arrangements
- ✓ Test the student understanding of topic
- ✓ Notes will be provided by the Teacher
- ✓ Use Tape Recorder
- ✓ Oral Test

Modifications on IEP are changing the curriculum to meet the needs of the student's level of ability.

**IEP Modifications For ADHD**

- Word bank for vocabulary word banks
- Less homework problems to do
- Projects instead of written reports
- Reworded Questions in simpler language

**Examples of IEP Goals And Objectives**

**Functional Behavior And Behavior Intervention Plan:**

I see children having a hard time self-regulating their emotions in school. Many times, children are being suspended because they threaten another child or want to blow up the building.

If you do not have a Behavior Intervention Plan on your IEP, then request to have an IEP meeting to have your child evaluated for his behavior issues.

The school will do a Functional Behavior Assessment. A Functional Behavior Assessment (FBA) is a tool that psychologist or Behavior Specialist.

This is a process that they will document what becomes before the behavior (antecedent), the behavior the child is showing, and what happens after the behavior(consequences).

They accumulate this data from observing the child in classroom and interview the parents and teachers to see why the bad behavior is occurring.

They can collect data for two to three weeks. Once they have the data and decide what is causing the behavior issues, then they will put together with the IEP team a behavior Intervention plan.   (Mauro, 2011)

Self Help Guide to ADHD and ADD

**Example of FBA:**

## FUNCTIONAL BEHAVIORAL ASSESSMENT (FBA)

Student:_______________________ Grade________ School:__________________________________ Date:___________

Participants: _______________________________________________________________________

This FBA will be utilized for:　☐ Programming purposes　☐ IEP requirements

| **1** Describe the behavior/incident in observable terms: | **4** ANTECEDENTS | **5** CONSEQUENCES |
|---|---|---|
| | What is likely to "set off" or precede the problem behavior? **WHEN** is the problem behavior most likely to occur? | What "payoff" does the student obtain when she/he demonstrates the problem behavior? |
| | ☐ Morning — approximate time(s) ____________<br>☐ Afternoon — approximate time(s) ____________<br>☐ Before/after school　☐ Lunch/recess<br>☐ *Time of day does not seem to affect this behavior* | The student **GAINS**:<br>☐ Teacher/adult attention<br>☐ Peer attention<br>☐ Desired item or activity<br>☐ Control over others or situation<br>☐ Self Stimulation<br>☐ ________________________ |
| | **WHERE** is the problem most likely to occur?<br>☐ Reg. Ed. classroom　☐ Spec. Ed. classroom<br>☐ Hallways　☐ Cafeteria<br>☐ ____________________<br>☐ *Location does not seem to affect this behavior* | |
| | During what **SUBJECT/ACTIVITY** is the problem behavior most likely to occur?<br>☐ Subject(s)____________________<br>☐ Unconstructed activities　☐ Seatwork<br>☐ Group Activities　☐ Transitions<br>☐ Lesson presentations　☐ Task explanations<br>☐ ____________________<br>☐ *Subject/activity does not seem to affect this behavior* | The student **AVOIDS** or **ESCAPES**:<br>☐ Teacher/adult attention<br>☐ Peer attention<br>☐ Non-preferred activity, task or setting<br>☐ A difficult task or frustrating situation<br>☐ ________________________ |
| **2** If the above statement addresses multiple behaviors, identify the **ONE BEHAVIOR** to be targeted for intervention:<br>____________________<br>____________________<br>____________________<br>____________________<br>____________________ | The **PEOPLE** that are present when the problem behavior is most likely to occur include:<br>☐ Teacher　☐ Classmates<br>☐ Other Staff　☐ Other peers<br>☐ ____________________<br>☐ *Subject/activity does not seem to affect this Behavior* | What has been tried thus far to change the problem behavior?<br>☐ This is a first occurrence and will be addressed through this FBA and Behavior Intervention Plan.<br>☐ Implemented rules and consequences for behavior are posted.<br>☐ Implemented behavior or academic contract.<br>☐ Implemented home/school communication system.<br>☐ Adapted curriculum — How? ____________ |
| | Are there **OTHER EVENTS** or **CONDITIONS** that immediately precede the problem behavior?<br>☐ A demand or request<br>☐ Unexpected changes in schedule or routine<br>☐ Consequences imposed for behavior<br>☐ Comments/teasing from other students<br>☐ ____________________ | ☐ Modified instruction — How? ____________ |
| **3** Other medical/mental conditions that may contribute to target behavior: ____________<br>____________________<br>____________________<br>____________________<br>____________________ | When is the student most successful? When **DOESN'T** the problem behavior occur? ____________<br>____________________<br>____________________<br>____________________<br>____________________ | ☐ Adjusted schedule — How? ____________<br><br>☐ Conference with parents — Dates? ____________<br><br>☐ Sent student to office — Dates? ____________ |

**Behavioral Intervention Plan**

A Behavior Intervention Plan is used to teach and reinforce positive behaviors. Typically, a child's IEP team develops the plan. It usually includes:
- Skills training to increase appropriate behavior
- Changes that will be made in classrooms or other environments to reduce and eliminate problem behaviors.

Why does a child show bad behavior?

- Escape/ avoidance
- Attention
- Expression of anger
- Frustration
- Seeking power / control
- Intimidation
- Sensory stimulation
- Relief of fear or anxiety
- Peer acceptance

## Suspensions From School:

Many children from kindergarten to middle school are getting suspended because he or she have threatened to blow up the school or hit another peer in class.

Schools can suspend a child with a disability for up to 10 consecutive days (10 days in a row) for any violation of a school rule as long as that it is the same disciplinary action (and amount) applied to children without disabilities, except if the offense involves weapons, drugs or serious bodily injury.

If your child has been suspended, I would ask to set up an IEP meeting with the IEP team so they can do a Functional Behavior Assessment and get a Behavioral Intervention Plan in place so they can provide the strategy to manage his behavior.

Self Help Guide to ADHD and ADD

Example of Behavioral Intervention Plan:

## Behavioral Intervention Plan

Date: __2/1/98__

Student Name: __Case 3 - Ed__     ID: __0003__     DOB: __5/3/82__     Case Manager: __Mr. Roberts__

| Behavior Number(s) | Expected Outcome(s) Goal(s) | Intervention(s) & Frequency of Intervention | Person Responsible | Goal/Intervention Review Notes |
|---|---|---|---|---|
| 1 | A. During free time, interacts with other students and staff 90% of the time.<br><br>B. Goes to lunch in the cafeteria without supervision 90% of the time.<br><br>C. On task 90% of the time.<br><br>D. Completes assigned work 90% of the time. | A. Social work involvement for referral for family counseling focused on realistic expectations of student performance. Ongoing until counseling is started.<br><br>B. Daily monitoring medication compliance and effectiveness.<br><br>C. Bibliotherapy for parents. Ongoing.<br><br>D. Teach the student alternative positive self-statements and appraisals. Daily, as needed.<br><br>E. Reinforce positive self-statements, attention to school work, and initiating social interactions. Daily, as needed<br><br>F. Weekly group instruction of combating irrational and self defeating thinking in special education classroom. | Social worker<br><br>Nurse, Teacher<br><br>Parents<br><br>Teacher<br><br>Teacher<br><br>Teacher | 4/1/98 - Showing improvement to 60% on Goal A. Showing improvement on Goals C and D. Little change in Goal B. Social worker made contact with parents, but they are resistant. Continue efforts on Intervention A and C. Intervention F seems to be very effective. Need to increase treatment integrity on Intervention E. Goal B is unique that it is not in the classroom. Need to interview student to better understand social problems outside of class. |

* Review Codes: GA - Goal Achieved | C - Continue | DC - Discontinue     Expected Review Dates: __4/1/98__ | __5/1/98__ | __________

Signatures: __________________ __________________ __________________ __________________

__________________ __________________ __________________ __________________

## Multidisciplinary Evaluation Team (MET)

The evaluation team will complete the evaluation and determine the student's eligibility for special education within 60 calendar days from the date on which the parents provided informed written consent or the date on which the parents provided a written request for an evaluation.

A team is put together to see if your son or daughter has a disability and therefore will qualify for special education services. They will review their strengthens and weakness of your child, academics test results, medical history, review any school records. Once the report is complete, they will have a meeting with the results of the MET.

## Your Rights

When an evaluation is conducted, you have the right to:

- Give written approval before your student is evaluated (Referral/Evaluation Review/Consent form).
- Have an evaluation conducted by a multi-disciplinary evaluation team within 30 school days after the school has received your written permission to evaluate.

- Have more than one test or evaluation procedure used to determine eligibility and the appropriate education program for your student.
- Be assured that testing does not discriminate on the basis of language or culture.
- Have outside evaluation data considered along with school data.
- Be notified of each evaluation procedure, test, record, or report the IEP Team uses in determining eligibility and the need for special education programs or services.
- Have a re-evaluation every three years or more frequently, if requested. Receive copies of evaluation report prior to meeting.

### Behavior Intervention Plan

A behavior Intervention plan have goals and strategies that will provide prompts, so the child is reinforced with positive behavior. They must set a measurable goal so that you know that the strategies are working or not.

Some Behavior Goals on an IEP would be as follow:

- David will interact with his peer in a positive manner 8 out 10 times.
- Gerry will raise his hand before speaking in class 8 out 10 times or 70%
- Teresa will use appropriate language at all times and will show self-control 80%.
- Alex will show 80% of the time good problem-solving skills in class.
- Sandy will request a break when frustrated or upset by using the break card or verbalizing his needs 80% of the time.

# Behavioral Intervention Plan

Date: 2/1/98

Student Name: Case 3 - Ed      ID: 0003      DOB: 5/3/82      Case Manager: Mr. Roberts

| Behavior Number(s) | Expected Outcome(s) Goal(s) | Intervention(s) & Frequency of Intervention | Person Responsible | Goal/Intervention Review Notes |
|---|---|---|---|---|
| 1 | A. During free time, interacts with other students and staff 90% of the time.<br><br>B. Goes to lunch in the cafeteria without supervision 90% of the time.<br><br>C. On task 90% of the time.<br><br>D. Completes assigned work 90% of the time. | A. Social work involvement for referral for family counseling focused on realistic expectations of student performance.  Ongoing until counseling is started.<br><br>B. Daily monitoring medication compliance and effectiveness.<br><br>C. Bibliotherapy for parents. Ongoing.<br><br>D. Teach the student alternative positive self-statements and appraisals.  Daily, as needed.<br><br>E. Reinforce positive self-statements, attention to school work, and initiating social interactions. Daily, as needed<br><br>F. Weekly group instruction of combating irrational and self defeating thinking in special education classroom. | Social worker<br><br><br>Nurse,<br>Teacher<br><br>Parents<br><br>Teacher<br><br>Teacher<br><br><br>Teacher | 4/1/98 - Showing improvement to 60% on Goal A.  Showing improvement on Goals C and D.  Little change in Goal B.  Social worker made contact with parents, but they are resistant. Continue efforts on Intervention A and C. Intervention F seems to be very effective.  Need to increase treatment integrity on Intervention E. Goal B is unique that it is not in the classroom. Need to interview student to better understand social problems outside of class. |

* Review Codes: GA = Goal Achieved | C = Continue | DC = Discontinue      Expected Review Dates: 4/1/98 | 5/1/98 | _______

Signatures: _______________________________________________________________

_______________________________________________________________

## Transitioning Services Out Of High School

One of the questions that parents always ask me when I am doing my workshops is Why worry about the Transitioning services out of high school?

It is very critical that you start to see what areas your child needs help with in school. Many of us take it day by day with our children needs and before you know it, they are walking across the stage getting their diploma and we start asking them what do you want to do with yourself when you graduate.

There has been research that students with disabilities are significantly unemployed and underemployed upon leaving school compared to their nondisabled peers.

Children who have disabilities will leave school without successfully earning any type of diploma. Statistics show that adults with disabilities earn less income then nondisabled adults. (New Era, 2002)

Schools are not doing a good job providing transition services to children who have disabilities. Parents leave it up to the schools to provide the services they feel their child needs to succeed in school.

Transition Services can be defined as strategies, services and activities that will achieve a smooth transition to post-secondary school or getting a job when they graduate from college.

Under the IDEA 2004 transition services will occur when the student turns 16 or earlier if the IEP Team determines that is necessary for that particular student.

There are three areas that the transition services will focus on when we are developing these measurable goals in your child's IEP.

- Training and Education
- Employment
- Independent Living Skills

## Training And Education

Some of the things your child needs to think about is what they are going to do when they graduate from High School. Do they want to attend a two-year college or four-year-old college? Do they want to go into the Military or start working full time?

One of the goals you will see on their IEP for Training and Education is as follow:

Johnny will be enrolled at Chandler Gilbert Community College Full-time in the Computer Science program.

**Employment**

Another choice your child has when they graduate from school is to work full-time.  On your IEP you will see a goal for employment as follow:

After graduation David will work full-time as a secretary in a law office.

After graduation Phil will attend on the job training program learning about plumbing.

**Independent Living**

Cindy will live in an apartment with a roommate after she graduates from High School.

Dan will learn how to take the bus from his apartment to his work

**Transition Assessments**

In order for teenagers making a decision on their careers and education there are formal and informal assessments that they can participate in high school.

**Formal Assessments**

- Standardized achievement tests
- Intellectual functioning assessment
- Aptitude tests
- Personality scales
- Interest Inventories

**Informal Assessments**

- Interest inventories
- Skills inventories
- Situational observations
- Situational assessments
- Interviews
- Curriculum-based assessments

You know your child better than anybody, so I want you to ask questions about the transition process. Speak up in the IEP meeting if you know that this would not be attainable for your child and do not put off tomorrow what you can do today.

Transiting out of high school starts when they are sixteen years old or sooner. Be realistic with your expectations for your child capabilities.

I see kids struggle with money management, setting up their own doctors' appointments, washing clothes, or making a meal for themselves.

If I were you, I would start these accomplishments when they start their freshman year in High School. These are some of the responsibilities we have as parents that needs to be address before they graduate high school.

## Money Management

Why should children learn about money management now?

First, teenagers need to get into good habits, so they won't have financial problems.

Secondly, down the road they will have to make good buying decisions making long term purchases such as a car or attaining a student loan for college.

It's important that they do not get stuck in the pitfalls of high interest loans that can get you deeply into debt.

### Credit Card vs. Debit Card

Many teenagers today get confused with the difference between a credit card and debit card. It's up to us as parents to educate our sons and daughters about these concepts so they do not accumulate outrageous overdraft charges and debt that could create financial problems for you.

Credit Card is a card that can be used to buy goods and services on a certain amount of money that is issued by the bank, savings and loans, retail businesses.

Debit Card is a card the banks provide access to their funds immediately. Unlike Credit cards that floats you some money. Debit cards will be charged over drafted fees if there are no funds to cover their purchases. This is a hard lesson for teenagers to spend their money with in a budget. Over drafted fees can add up very quickly.

Suggestions I have for parents is to provide your child with a budget each month. Allow them to get a job for 10 hours a week.

Provide them with a folder to keep all their receipts in and review each week if it was a need or want. Ask how they can improve on their buying decisions. This teaches them responsibility and independence.

Another suggestion for this lesson on budgeting is to sit down with your personal finances on a weekly basis and show them the cost of mortgage, insurances, food, TV, internet, cell phones etc.

You will be amazed how clueless teenagers can be when it comes to making purchases.

## Credit Scores

An individual's credit score affects his or her ability to borrow money through financial institutions.

Your interest rates and credit limits are based on how quickly you pay your bills.

When you are searching for insurances and employment, they will run a credit report to see if your child is in good standings.

This is something teenagers need to understand when they are getting credit cards and paying their bills.

## Credit Score Ratings

- Excellent (750-850)
- Good (660-749)
- Fair (620-659)
- Poor (314 -619)

## Thief Identity

- Many individuals Identity is being taken by doing transaction on the computer, atm etc.
- Check your credit cards monthly and make sure that there are no additional charges being charged at your account.
- Children need to be aware if someone is using their credit card.  They will need to call up the credit card company to cancel their card.
- Do not leave wallets or purses in the car.

## Short Vs. Long Term Gratification

I feel we need to show our children the difference between short term and long-term gratification. Many of our children want instant gratification instead of working for something long term.

This is a very good concept to start early in life since they need to understand about how they will need to save up for retirement.

One of the things I did for my son was to set up a traditional IRA at his bank so he could deposit a certain amount each month out of his paycheck so the time he retires he would have great start when he has no financial responsibilities.

I wish I did this when I started to work but my parents never sat down with me to talk about retirement.

## Medication

Amphetamine Stimulants
- Adderall   Short-acting          4-6 hours
- Adderall XR  Long-acting        8-12 hours
- Vyvanse        Long-acting      10-12 hours
- Ritalin  Short-acting           3-4 hours
- Concerta Long-acting            10-12 hours

Non-stimulants
- Strattera (atomoxetine) Long-acting (extended release)24 hours
- IntunivLong-acting (extended release)24 hours

Sleepiness, headache, fatigue, abdominal pain. Rarely, Intuniv can cause low pressure and heart rhythm changes.

Some loss of appetite, weight loss, sleep problems, irritability, tics. Longer-acting medicines are convenient but may have greater side effects on appetite and sleep.

## Holistic Treatment For ADHD

### Bio Feedback

EEG Biofeedback therapy involves placing one or more sensors on the scalp and one to each ear. These sensors are then connected to a device records the electrical activity of the brain, referred to as brain waves.

From the EEG, the therapist helps the client to associate specific mental states with his/her brain waves. Feedback regarding brain activity is presented to the client via a video game in which the brightness and speed of a Pacman like figure corresponds to a preset threshold.

The therapist guides the client by telling him/her to make the video game work with his/her brain.

My son did this a few times and felt good but the cost is very expensive. $100 per session with an estimation for treatment would be between $2000-$4000.

You would have to check with your Medical insurance provider would cover this type of treatment.

LearningRX Center was done on my child and they did an evaluation on his intellectual behavior. There are several brain trainings franchises throughout the United States that specialize in this area of expertise.

When I took my son to the LearningRX, I wanted to see what they could do for him since he had troubles with concentration, and memorization. They evaluated him on his reading, writing, and math. Our son would go twice a week to have one on one training session with a tutor.

Their focus was to increase his memorization and improve on his concentration. I found this to be very helpful and saw some positive results in school. (Gibson,Hanson,Mitchell,&Tepas2019)

www.learningrx.com

## Critical Thinking And Problem-Solving Skills

Many children with ADHD do not have the skills for critical thinking and problem solving. I believe like anything you do if you are not good at something the only way of improving is by practicing.

There is a company called critical thinking. They have books and CD's to improve these skills. You can go to www.critcalthinking.com to buy these products online.

## Talents

All children have special talents that need to be noticed and nurtured, so they will do well in school and in their daily lives.

Parents have an important role in helping their children develop these talents by working with them at home.

Talents can be defined as being good at a sport, playing a musical instrument, having the ability to be kind and funny.

These are a few suggestions that can help you see what talents your child have in themselves. Whatever talents your child has been given, praise them for it when you catch them in the moment.

Teachers should have an awareness of these talents to motivate and build your child's self-esteem in school. (Eric Putnam,2010)

## Self Esteem and Motivation in Children

I feel it is important for parents to have an awareness of our children's self-esteem.

Many children that have ADHD or ADD get picked on and bully at school. As a mother who has an ADHD child, I am concern he will have low self-esteem.

He has a difficult time making friends because of his weakness in socializing. I make sure he is involved in sports, boys' scouts, chess, and other events that he excels in to improve his confidence and social skills.

Also, I would praise him for his academic's achievements or his accomplishments in drawing or music to boost his self-esteem.

Self-esteem is the way we feel about ourselves. I think it's important for parents to encourage positive feeling in our children.

When I hear my son say he is stupid, or he cannot make friends, I tell him we all have things to improve about ourselves.

Remember, to have the I can do attitude and drill it into them until they start believing. The only way a child or ourselves can increase our self-esteem is by doing.

I would provide chores list or make him set the table, even assist me in my social skills group to build his self-esteem.

Motivation can be difficult if children do not want to try something new. ADHD or ADD children like to stay in routine and not venture out of their comfort zone.

I would make my son go to birthday parties and sports events to get him out to socialize.

If he needs some motivation, I would set up a rewards system to have him do his homework or behave in a positive manner.

These rewards will depend on the age of the child. Some parents believe kids should not be rewarded all the time to do what's expected of them.

I believe if it motivates him to be positive and do the right thing, I am fine with it. Once he learns the right behavior or make better choices I would back off on the rewards.

## Diet and Drinks

I know that diet and sugar drinks can affect a child's behavior. These are common sense things we have been hearing since we were kids.

Diet alone is not going to get rid of ADHD, ADD, Asperger's Syndrome or Autism. There are many factors why children have these disabilities today.

I blame it on the environment, the food we eat, immunizations and genetics. There is not one element that is causing the increase in ADHD and ADD.

I believe we can help our children in improving their temperament by watching what they put into their bodies.

As parents we can monitor the amounts of sugar and carbohydrates that they intake on a daily basis.

Everything should be done in moderation when it comes to food.  Some kids need to eat smaller meals because they burn through food quickly.

Hyperglycemic children will have their sugar up and down so if they try to eat less sugar and carbohydrates in their diet and smaller meals this could help them with their bad behavior.

Some doctors recommend for us to eat organic food to get more nutrients in our diet.  I try to eat as health as possible but it's difficult when we are on the go so much.

Many doctors that I have visited which were holistic or naturopathic have recommended taking a multiple vitamin.

Our diets are lacking protein, magnesium, folic acid, omega 3, and zinc. Today, many children have sensory to foods they will not like the taste or texture of the vitamin.

My son would like to drink a shake so I would make a protein drink.

These drinks come in chocolate or vanilla and I add fruit to flavor it up for him.  Be careful on what brand you buy because some protein drinks are made for adults.

I started out with Ensure and then as my son got older, I gave him Isogonics.  There are energy drinks that are all natural like Vemma that I heard about from Dr. Oz on TV.

Vemma has no sugar or caffeine in it, but only comes in orange flavor. If your child has a dislike for orange drinks, then you might want to see if sprouts or other organic markets carry something similar in a different flavor.

Soda and sugar juices are the worst drinks we can give to our children who have behavior issues.

**Gluten Free Food**

I tried to put my son on a gluten free diet and found it impossible to do. He didn't like the taste of the bland food.

Many children can get tested for gluten by taking a blood test. I believe you need to give it a try if your child is constipated and has stomach ache when he eats wheat products.

You can be sensitive to gluten products and have test results say that you don't. Speaking from experience with myself, I tested positive with Gluten free.

I feel better when I do not eat a lot of carbs in my diet. You need to read the labels on boxes, cans, and packages.

Sprouts and Whole Foods are located on the west coast has all their products marked Gluten free. I find them very pricey but well worth the benefit if I don't eat wheat in my diet.

I would try this for a few months with your child and see if he is feeling better or not.

## Conclusion

I hope this self-help guide was informative and resourceful to you. I am not a psychologist, physician or therapist, but a parent who is on this ADHD journey.

I know how it feels to fight for services in your school district, and the frustration working with your spouse or significant other who may feel differently about being diagnosis with ADHD and ADD.

Nobody knows your child better than you. This ADHD and ADD journey will continue into adulthood. The only way we can set our children up for success is by providing extra support in the home, school, and seeking outside community organizations services to support our children needs.

## Resources For Parents

Books to read
- ✓ Emotional Intelligence by Daniel Goldman
- ✓ Raising Social IQ Stepping stone to people skill for kids by Cathi Cohen
- ✓ Out of Sync child by Carol Stock Kranowicz
- ✓ 123 Magic by Phelan
- ✓ The Gift of ADHD- by Lara Hara-Webbs
- ✓ Six type of ADD by Daniel Amen

## Exhibit 1: Homework Chart

**Homework Assignment Sheet**

| Subject | Description | Page# | Completed |
|---|---|---|---|
| Math | | | |
| English | | | |
| Reading | | | |
| Science | | | |
| Social Studies | | | |

## Exhibit 2: Graphic Organizer

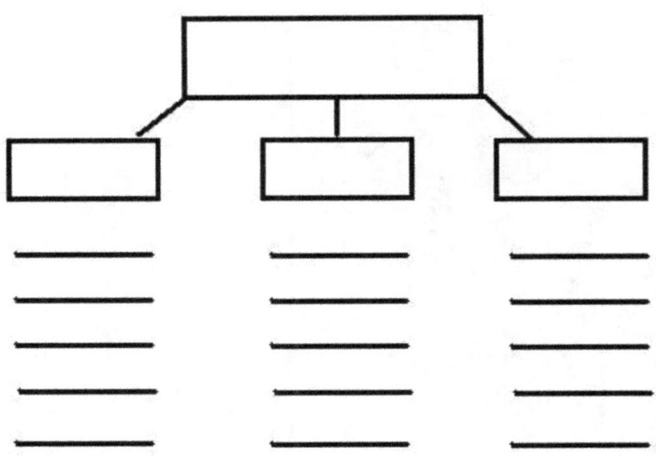

## Exhibit 3 : Venn Diagram

## Comparing and Contrasting

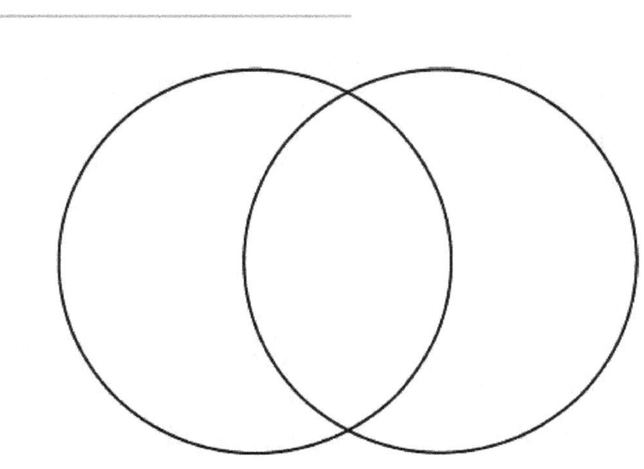

## Exhibit 4: Letter to Requesting Evaluation

Your Name
Street Address
City, State, Zip Code
Daytime telephone number


Name of Principal or Special Education Administrator
Name of School
Street Address
City, State, Zip Code


Dear (Principal's or Administrator's name),

I am writing to request that my son/daughter, (child's name), be evaluated for special education services. I am worried that (child's name) is not doing well in school and believe he/she may need special services in order to learn. (Child's name) is in the ( _ ) grade at (name of school). (Teacher's name) is his/her teacher.

Specifically, I am worried because (child's name) does/does not (give a few direct examples of your child's problems at school).

Thank you for your prompt attention to my request.


Sincerely,


Your name


cc: your child's principal (if letter is addressed to an administrator your child's teacher(s)

## Exhibit 5 IEP Need Analysis

**Eligibility:**
- ☐ Autism
- ☐ Multiple Disabilities
- ☐ Developmental Delay (ages 3-10) Multiple Disabilities Severe Sensory Impairment
- ☐ Emotional Disability Orthopedic Impairment
- ☐ Hearing Impairment Preschool Severe Delay
- ☐ Other Health Impairments –
  - ☐ ADHD
  - ☐ Speech/Language Impairment
  - ☐ Specific Learning Disability Traumatic Brain Injury
  - ☐ Visual Impairment

**Academic Learning problems**
- ☐ Math problems
- ☐ Sight words
- ☐ Writing

**Attention Issues:**
- ☐ Take test in quiet room
- ☐ study skills/organization skills
- ☐ Daydreaming
- ☐ Going from one task to another
- ☐ Short term memory

**Audio Processing**
- ☐ Re-direction with instruction
- ☐ Reading Comprehensive

**Body**
- ☐ Cannot stand someone touching them
- ☐ Need to be hugged
- ☐ Cannot stand clothes or socks on them
- ☐ Walking on their toes

**Behavior Issues**
- ☐ Aggressive- overly Explosive
- ☐ Anxiety
- ☐ Controlling
- ☐ Fixation on items
- ☐ Easily Frustrated
- ☐ Repetitive activities or motions
- ☐ Meltdowns or Tantrums
- ☐ Cannot regulate emotions
- ☐ Coping skills

**Coordination**
- ☐ Clumsy, trips, runs into things
- ☐ Slumps
- ☐ Hard to run

**Food problems**
- ☐ Gag on different textures
- ☐ Issues with Smells of perfumes, meat, house products

## Hyperactivity

- ☐ Climbing on furniture
- ☐ Cannot sit still

## Impulsiveness

- ☐ Talking out loud
- ☐ Cannot take turns
- ☐ Hits or touch people
- ☐ Chew things
- ☐ Cannot stand getting dirty
- ☐ Problem Solving

## Sensory Issues

### Visual

- ☐ Flipping of letters and words
- ☐ Copy from board to paper
- ☐ Can't make eye contact

### Audio

- ☐ Loud Noises
- ☐ Delay in responding to instruction

## Social Skills

- ☐ Joining in
- ☐ Taking turns
- ☐ Delay in Verbal Communication
- ☐ Nonverbal communication
- ☐ Teasing
- ☐ Resolving Conflicts

## Speech

- ☐ Nonverbal- understanding social cues
- ☐ Verbal cannot talk clear

Self Help Guide to ADHD and ADD

## Exhibit 6: IEP Binder information:

| Section 1—IEP / 504 Plan | Section 2—Assessments (Child Study Team) | Section 3—Independent Evaluations | Section 4—Correspondences to School | Section 5—Correspondences from school |
|---|---|---|---|---|
| **Child's** most current SIGNED IEP or 504. | | | | |
| All other **IEP's** should be filed away in a separate binder as reference. | _Educational | **Child's** profile "successes" | _ Document phone calls | _ Document phone calls |
| Suggest current and previous year of the IEP. | _ Functional | What they can do vs. what they need help doing. | _ Letters | _ Letters |
| | _ Social | | _ E-mails | _ E-mails |
| | _ Psychological | | _ Notes | _ Notes |
| | _ Speech | | | |
| | _ Occupational Therapy | | | |
| | _ Physical Therapy | | | |

## Exhibit 7:  Parent Transition Survey

Student: _______________________________

Date: _________________________________


Please add any comments or concerns that you feel will assist the IEP team in making decisions for the Individual Education Program (IEP). (Fournier, L.L. M.E. Morningstar, I. Crawford, J. Scarff & M. Blue-Banning, 2014).

### Area 1: Post-Secondary Education

My son/daughter intends to go on to post-secondary education or training as indicated:
_____ 4-year College _____ Community College
_____ Vocational/Technical School _____ Other
_____ My son/daughter does not intend to go on to post-secondary education

___________________________________________

Comments_____________________________________


### Area 2: Vocational Training

My son/daughter has successfully completed course work in the following vocational areas:
_____ Family and Consumer Sciences
_____ Computers
_____ Construction Trades
_____ Business

_____ Health Studies
_____ Industrial Arts
_____ Photography
_____ Graphic Arts
_____ Auto
_____ Other:

---

**Area 3:  Career And Employment**

My son/daughter has had the following work experiences:
_____ Volunteer employment _____ Full or part-time employment
_____ On the Job training
_____ Military

My son/daughter requires IEP team assistance in the following areas:
_____ Career exploration
_____ Identification of personal interests, values, and skills
_____ Career planning
_____ Conducting a job search
_____ Completing applications for employment
_____ Job interviewing skills
_____ Preparing resumes

_____Developing pre-employment behaviors: following directions, staying on task, completing tasks, locating materials, dress and grooming issues, etc.

_____Developing employment behaviors: attendance, punctuality, use of equipment, independent work habits, completing assigned tasks accurately, increasing productivity, etc.

_____ On the job training with a job coach

_____ Other:

Comments:__________________________________

## Area 4: Continuing And Adult Education

My son/daughter requires assistance from the IEP Team in the following:

_____Identifying possible continuing education options

_____Information about Adult Education Programs

_____Information about GED Preparation Programs

_____ Referral to an adult agency for continuing education

_____ Other

Comments:__________________________________

## Area 5: Adult Services

My son/daughter is currently connected to the following community agencies:
_____Division of Vocational Rehabilitation (DVR)
_____Division of Developmental Disabilities Services (DDDS)
_____Social Security Administration
_____Other

_______________________________________

My son/daughter requires IEP Team assistance in the following:
_____Identifying appropriate agencies for support services
_____Referral to an adult service provider
_____Assistance in completing an application for services
_____Other
Comments:_______________________________

_______________________________________

## Area 6: Independent Living Skills

My son/daughter has age appropriate skills in the following areas:
_____ Budgeting
_____ Maintenance of a household
_____ Cooking
_____ Self-help (grooming, dress, hygiene)
_____ Communication skills

Self Help Guide to ADHD and ADD

_____ Recreation/leisure skills
_____ Community safety
_____ Caring for personal health
_____ Accessing medical assistance
_____ Self-advocacy
_____ Shopping
_____ Money skills
_____ Use of banking services
_____ Use of credit
_____ Accessing transportation services
_____ Personal relationships
_____ Caring for others (babysitting, parents)
_____Making friends
_____Accessing community services
_____Other_______________________________________

_______________________________________

My son/daughter needs IEP Team assistance in the following areas:
_____Money management (banking, credit, budgeting)
_____Personal care (dress, grooming, hygiene)
_____Household management (bills, rent, household maintenance, cleaning, etc.)
_____Community safety
_____Personal relationships (making friends, sex education, etc.)
_____Caring for others (parenting skills, family relationships, dating, marriage)

_____Communication skills

_____Social skills

_____Recreation/Leisure skills

_____Shopping Skills

_____Self Advocacy (accessing assistance in legal, medical, financial areas)

_____ Other

## Area 7: Recreational Activities

My son/daughter accesses the following community organizations:

_____Religious organization of choice

_____Athletic club

_____Hobbies, and interest

_____Swimming

_____School athletics/clubs/extracurricular activities

_____Other

My son/daughter uses the following transportation:

_____Drives self

_____Community public transportation

_____Taxi service

_____Bicycle

_____Walks

My son/daughter needs IEP Team assistance in the following areas:

____Identifying community organizations and activities

____Participating in school activities

____Using community skills

____Developing recreation/leisure skills

____Referral to a community service provider

____Other

Comments:

---

## References


A New Era: Revitalizing Special Education for Children and Their Families, July 2002. From: http://ectacenter.org/~pdfs/calls/2010/earlypart c/revitalizing_special_education.pdf

Bridger, D., (2008). Boost your Memory, infinite ideas limited, United Kingdom.

CHADD. (2012) Children and Adults with Attention-Deficit/Hyperactivity Disorder Understanding ADHD. Retrieved on October 11, 2011 From: http://www.chadd.org/Content/CHADD/Understanding/Symptoms/

Cohen, C., (2000). Raising Your Children Social IQ Stepping Stones to People Skills For Kids. Advantage Books, MD.

Ehmke, R., (2019). Helping Kids who struggle with Executive Functions. Retrieve on 9th, June 2019 From: https://childmind.org/article/helping-kids-who-struggle-with-executive-functions .

Encyclopedia Children's Health (2012) Psychological Tests - meaning, Definition, Purpose, Description, Risks. Retrieved9, January2012, from http://www.healthofchildren.com/P/Psychological-Tests.html#b#ixzz1luqaFJXI

English as 2nd Language (2012). Retrieved August 10, 2012 From: http://esl.about.com/od/writinglessonpla2/ig/Graphic-Organizers/Structured-Overview.htm

Franz, C., (2019). Mind mapping Retrieved from http://www.mymindmap.net/Mind_Map_Templates.html

Fournier, L.L. (Revised 2014). Parent Transition Survey. From Parent Transition Survey by M.E. Morningstar, I. Crawford, J. Scarf & M. Blue-Banning (1994). Adapted with permission. Retrieved From: http: transitioncoalition.org

Fuerst, M., (2016, August). Impact of ADHD Treatment on Risky Behaviors, Child Adolescent Psychiary retrieve from https://www.psychiatrictimes.com.

Gibson, Hanson, Mitchell and, Tenpas (2019, June 29). *ADHD*. Retrieved from https://www.learningrx.com/

Ghose, T., (2013) http://ca.news.yahoo.com/simple-vision-test-predicts-iq-160717367.html

Mauro, T., (2011) Behavior intervention plan; children with special needs. About.com. Retrieved, From:http://specialchildren.about.com/od/beharanddiscipline/g/BIP.htm .

McKissick, G., Palacios, M., Rodriguez, E., Segura. L. (2000), Spanish Articulation/ Phonology Program. Retrieved From: https://springscs.org/wp-content/uploads/2014/09/oral_motor_speech_exercises.pdf

Memorial Hospital, Inc. (2005). Parent's Guide to Understanding Sensory. Retrieved October 11, 2011. From: http://memorialhospital.org/SensoryIntegration.htm

Putnam, E., (2010, August) Challenge temperaments, Independence Behavior Coaching.

Siegel, M. L., (2011) The Complete IEP guide how to advocate for your special ed child. 7th edition. Nolo Trademark, CA.

Stokes, S., (1999-2011). Examples of IEP Goals and Objectives Suggestions for Autism children. Cooperative Education Services, Agency No.7, WI Retrieved 09, February 2012. From: http://www.specialed.us/autism/05/g_o.htm.

The American Academy of Child and Adolescent Psychiatry (AACAP) Children with ODD, (2010) "Facts for Families" No.72 (3/11) Washington D.C. Retrieved on February 22, 2012 from http://www.aacap.org/galleries

Wilbarger, P., MED, OTR and Wilbarger, J. L. MS, OTR (2001). "Sensory Defensiveness in Children Aged 2-12, An Intervention Guide for Parents and Other Caretakers" Avanti Educational Programs.

Notes:

Notes:

Notes: